Innocent Vic~~tims~~

ABOUT THE AUTHOR

At the time of his appointment to the NSPCC, Dr Alan Gilmour was Deputy Secretary of the British Medical Association, Treasurer of the Association for the Study of Medical Education and a Vice-President of the Section of Medical Education of the Royal Society of Medicine.

He was appointed Director of the NSPCC in 1979. He seized on the opportunity of the Society's Centenary in 1984 to achieve a restructuring of its services to abused and neglected children that would ensure its continuing relevance to their needs. The Society is now entering its second century with a larger task force of 'Inspectors', offering a focused and structured professional service through a network of Child Protection teams that work in close partnership with local authority social services throughout England, Wales and Northern Ireland.

Dr Gilmour who is 60, is married with two grown-up daughters. He was awarded the C.B.E. in the Queen's Birthday Honours in June 1984.

Innocent Victims
The Question of Child Abuse

Dr Alan Gilmour
Director of the National Society for the
Prevention of Cruelty to Children

Foreword by Esther Rantzen

MICHAEL JOSEPH   LONDON

In all cases quoted in this book that have not become public
knowledge through the reporting of trials and inquiries, names,
locations and other details have been changed to preserve confidentiality and so protect the children involved. But it is important to
stress that child abuse, in all forms, occurs throughout the country.

MICHAEL JOSEPH LTD
Published by the Penguin Group
27 Wrights Lane, London W8 5TZ, England
Viking Penguin Inc., 40 West 23rd Street, New York, New York 10010, USA
Penguin Books Australia Ltd, Ringwood, Victoria, Australia
Penguin Books Canada Ltd, 2801 John Street, Markham, Ontario, Canada
L3R 1B4
Penguin Books (NZ) Ltd, 182–190 Wairau Road, Auckland 10, New Zealand

Penguin Books Ltd, Registered Offices: Harmondsworth, Middlesex,
England

First published in Great Britain 1988

Copyright © Dr Alan Gilmour 1988 Director of the NSPCC

ISBN 0 7181 2958 X

Printed and bound in Great Britain by Richard Clay, Bungay, Suffolk
Filmset in Meridien by Cambrian Typesetters, Frimley, Surrey
A CIP catalogue record is available from the British Library

Contents

List of Illustrations

All photographs are the copyright of the NSPCC

Foreword

Cruelty to children makes us extremely angry. So it should, of course. There have been times and places when child slavery, child suffering were part of the structure of society – children worked the looms in factories, were forced to sweep chimneys, to work as prostitutes. Those days are long gone. We now expect children to be loved and cherished, to be properly educated and fed. When I, as a mother, think of the sights and sounds in my own life that fill my heart with joy, they are almost invariably connected with happy children – the sight of them skipping through buttercup fields in the sunlight – the sound of their bubbling laughter at the pantomime. No wonder when that image is replaced by the vision of a starving child, a child cowering from blows or subjected to the destructive torture of sexual abuse, our first reaction is anger.

It is justified anger, because cruelty to children produces life-long pain. I have met and corresponded with many adult victims who suffered cruelty all through their childhoods, but were never discovered or protected. These are the children who are not in this book, because the NSPCC, the police, the social services were never alerted, because no teacher, or doctor, relative or friend ever discovered the child's agony. Children are easy to intimidate into silence once they become accustomed to pain as an everyday experience. Lack of love soon creates in a child a feeling of worthlessness and guilt. The child comes to believe that, as one child wrote to me, 'It's my job to suffer'. When, as usually occurs, the cruelty is at the hands of one parent or both, the child will join a conspiracy to protect them. There must be an instinct in children that yearns for the ideal parent, the loving arms, the safe cuddle.

The shame and humiliation of a child who is the victim of neglect or violence will cause that child to try and conceal the bruises, deny the hunger. 'I used to skip P.E. lessons, so teacher wouldn't see where he'd hit me', 'I said I'd fallen downstairs', or 'I used to pretend to be like all my friends', many children have told me. The result is that the cruelty can continue for year after year, childhood can become a life sentence of pain for the child. And that in its turn creates a terribly damaged adult. Everything we know about tenderness, loyalty, compassion, caring, we learn first in our childhood, mainly from our parents. If instead they teach us pain, fear, betrayal, guilt, it must affect our own capacity to make relationships, to trust any other adult. A girl of sixteen wrote to me to describe the effects of the sexual abuse her stepfather had inflicted on her for eight years – 'I'm going to be lonely for the rest of my life. I know you're thinking I'll find someone to love, but I won't. If I meet a boy and he wants to take me out again I feel as though I've got to give him something and I've nothing left to give. I don't feel as though I deserve anyone who'll love me. I suppose happiness is an emotion I will never know. I think I was born to be hurt.'

This book is written from the clear standpoint that no child was born to be hurt, that every child has the right to happiness. But this is not a bill of children's rights, it is far more practical and valuable. It puts into perspective the horrific headlines that greet us every time another case of child abuse is discovered, because the NSPCC works, day-in-day-out, with cases that never make the headlines. And from its work, Dr Gilmour is able to answer some of the most crucial questions in child protection – how can we spot the abused children, how can we best help them? How can we analyse the causes of cruelty, and decide when a family can be supported and reconstructed, or when a child must be rescued and the abuser brought to justice? Dr Gilmour believes that more could, and should be done to save children from pain. The law at the moment so often merely forces abused children to endure still greater pain in the courtroom, without achieving justice or a conviction for the abuser. Dr Gilmour believes, as we at ChildLine believe, that the introduction of videotaped recordings of the interviews with abused children would be a major step forward. He also believes that the whole community has a role to play, the teachers, the doctors, the neighbours who live alongside these children but too often seem oblivious of their misery. He offers guidance in picking up the signs of abuse, and he maps the various kinds of action those who suspect cruelty should take. He does so fully aware that there is no ultimate solution to child abuse; we cannot drag the hands of the clock back and recreate a childhood with love instead of pain. The best we can do is strengthen the child, and the family, because as Dr Gilmour says, 'Child abuse is a family problem.'

Dr Gilmour knows too well that 'Child abuse work is difficult, demanding, emotionally stressful and often physically dangerous'. Those who are prepared to take it on must also accept that mistakes can lead to a lynch mob baying for blood, anyone's blood, but usually the social worker's or the NSPCC officer's.

Anger, though understandable, though justifiable, is the most destructive emotion if we really want to protect children. Dr Gilmour's book is never angry: he is compassionate, he is realistic. Instead of creating a gallery of monsters, his book is about human beings. The children are the innocent victims, but the abusers can be victims too. Many children who ring ChildLine refuse to identify themselves because they still deeply love and need the parents who cause them pain; the children know that calling for help may bring about the total destruction of their family. As one child told me, 'I don't want to hurt my brothers or break up my family so I have to put up with it till he drops down dead. I will be happy then. Please help the other children who are suffering. I am a stupid coward, no one can help me, it's my job now.' She was anonymous, dared not ask for help. Only by learning the lessons in this book, by controlling our anger and replacing it with Dr Gilmour's rational compassion can we discover and protect the children who believe they were born to be hurt, that it is their job to suffer.

ESTHER RANTZEN
June 1988

Author's Note

In writing this short account of child abuse and some of its related problems I make no pretence of producing a definitive textbook; rather my aim has been to give an informal chat. My purpose has been to try and describe the extent and nature of the problem, and to give some idea of what cruelty and neglect happens every day in all of our communities, and of the services which exist to protect and help children.

The views expressed are my own and reflect some of the key issues I have had to address during my time as Director of the NSPCC, but the experience on which they are based derives from the collective input of hundreds of people who have contributed to the work of the NSPCC. Some of my colleagues, notably Philip Noyes and Sue Creighton, have consciously contributed by reading parts of the text, by commenting on or verifying specific points, or by providing case histories; others have provided case histories from their experience; many unidentified workers have through their respective inputs into working to protect children helped to develop the basic corpus of knowledge and understanding which the NSPCC has achieved in over a hundred years of caring. There are too many to name individually, but I salute them all.

One person who has supported me throughout by commenting on the text, collating information and providing help and advice from his own rich professional experience is Robin Wratten, to whom I am particularly indebted. It is customary to thank whoever has painstakingly reproduced all of the typescript material, a task uncomplainingly carried out by my Amstrad word processor.

Introduction

Child abuse can happen in any kind of home, at any time and at any level of society. Every week children die in their own homes at the hands of those responsible for their care. Year by year, we see an increase in the thousands who suffer lesser levels of physical, mental or sexual assault, or neglect.

The only hope we can have is that this rise is due to better reporting, better discovery, of cruelty that already exists; and I believe that there is some truth in this, particularly in respect of the frightening rate of escalation of reports of child sexual abuse. However, nobody can be sure that the true rate of *incidence* of abuse might not be going up as well. That children are abused at all is of immense concern to us all; and the possibility that evil in our society is increasing is a disquieting thought that does not leave me.

What is child abuse? How does it happen? Why? Who is responsible for it? What is being done about it? Surely it can be prevented? Questions such as these race through the minds of all caring people when they are confronted with the evidence that so many children suffer, even in their very homes — the places where they should be safe. In the following chapters I shall try to share the answers, in so far as I can; that is, I shall describe the present state of knowledge of this scourge of the innocent which has been with mankind for so long.

Cruelty — 'man's inhumanity to man', as Burns declaimed in *Man was Made to Mourn* — is unlikely to be eliminated from mankind. Psychopathic or malignly evil torture is, mercifully, rare; but much harm can happen before its perpetrators can be removed from society once they have been identified. The often unintended hurts which come from physical (or other) acts of sudden anger will always be; the unexpected tragedy that results from some minor wrong cannot always be prevented. Nor is cruelty simply defined: for much of the suffering that affects the lives of tens of thousands of children constitutes a complex range of deprivation, mental anguish, bodily hurt and simple misery. And cruelty of any kind can occur in homes like yours or mine.

That is why I want to write about it. I do not intend to indulge in emotive sermonising – and I certainly do not want to pander to appetites for gory tales. I am writing this book because child abuse is a family problem.

Parents and other members of the family so often get caught up in problems that they do not understand; the Archbishop of Canterbury has referred to the fact that many abusing parents are victims just as much as their children. Parenting is the most important role most of us can perform – yet, undertaken with no help or preparation other than learning from our own children as we try to bring them up in the light of our own experience, it is the most difficult. In our consideration of child abuse we must always take into account the family context with all its pressures and difficulties.

Problems that affect a number of families are a concern of the whole community; and if they are to be tackled they need the attention of the whole community. If that attention is to be effective it needs to be based on knowledge of the facts and understanding of the underlying causes.

This need for knowledge applies to all of us. Social workers and others who specialise in preventing child abuse know more than I can tell them from their own direct experience. But there are many other professionals whose work brings children to them – they may not need these special skills, but they do need to be alert to the possibility of abuse in all their dealings, to know how to recognise it and to be aware of how to get their suspicions followed up so that there can be proper investigation by an expert and protection for the child concerned. This applies particularly to teachers and nursery workers who are with children so much of the time, and who can be best placed to spot worrying changes in behaviour and respond to them.

But child abuse is much too important a matter to be left only to the professionals. There will never be enough of them to go round and they cannot be with families all the time. Neighbours are better placed to do that, and neighbours have a very important part to play: one that is better realised in small communities and so often missing in the conurbations – for it is possible to be more lonely among the teeming throngs in a big city than almost anywhere else.

Neighbours have two roles to play. The first is the easier and, overall, the more important: it is, quite simply, to be neighbourly. To remember that children are the nation's most important investment and to help to make them safe, secure and able to develop their natural potential. This is not just a matter of being tolerant – which can be very difficult on occasion. It is more a matter of being ready to help young parents when they seem overburdened; of backing up a single parent and giving him or her a break.

The second role may be more difficult, but it may be vital – literally lifesaving. No one likes to be a Nosey Parker, to tell tales. But if a child is seldom seen outdoors, is wan, frightened, bruised or unhappy, there may be no one else who can save that child but a neighbour who cares enough to get in touch with professional help: the police in emergency, the local social services, or the NSPCC, whose nearest number is in every directory and who promise confidentiality.

We can all, then, play a part in promoting the protection of children from abuse and neglect. This book is based upon the experience of many who have spent their whole careers helping children and families, and I hope that it will help to provide perspectives and aid understanding for all sectors of the community.

Chapter One: **What is Child Abuse?**

'The faces change ... the bruises don't' was one of the most telling phrases that Saatchi & Saatchi produced during the 1984 centenary appeal of the NSPCC. For over one hundred years the battle against child cruelty has gone on: times have changed, but human nature hasn't, and man's capacity for inhumanity to man – and child – continues.

Life for a child should be a carefree, happy time – but for three-year-old Sarah it certainly wasn't. She was timid, shockingly inadequately dressed, thin and very underweight for her age. She didn't have a single toy to play with; indeed, she didn't know what play was. Nor did she even know that she had a name. Her parents only ever called 'Oi!' – 'Oi! You!' – and she came to think that Oi was her real name.

In time, neighbours in the area – a cathedral city in the south of England – who had been worrying about her, and talking amongst themselves as to what they could do, telephoned the NSPCC. That way they knew that their names would never be divulged, but that something would be done. Sure enough, an NSPCC Inspector called to see the family. Little Sarah rushed up to him and put her skinny little arms around him, sensing that here was somebody who cared and could be trusted.

He talked to the parents, looked around, saw Sarah's unkempt bedroom, bare of any comfort or plaything, and was appalled. He arranged for Sarah to be taken into care at once while a full investigation was made; neighbours were interviewed, the doctor and health visitor contacted, enquiries made of Social Services and any other people who might have knowledge of the family.

A typical story unfolded of a broken marriage, Sarah's mother marrying again and her child being resented and rejected by the stepfather. He was cruel, strong and capable of fearsome tempers. Mother was so frightened of him that she didn't dare to show that she cared for her child at all. But for caring neighbours Sarah might not be alive to tell the tale.

Sometimes when a child is committed to care, after a breathing space while the child is away, work can be done to help the parents to learn to cope and have their child back to a better standard of care in their home. But it was decided that Sarah's was not such a case: there just did not seem to be scope for improvement and the stepfather was not prepared to change his ways. For her own safety and well-being it was arranged for Sarah to continue in care, while the long slow process of helping her to recover from her unhappy and traumatic life could begin.

On another occasion a general practitioner contacted the Society: a young mother in a small town in mid-Wales had asked for help as she was having great difficulty in coping with her two daughters, aged four and six. She felt at the end of her tether, and when her nerves had finally cracked she had beaten the eldest girl in a way that had made her very worried and ashamed. The doctor felt that, while the girl was not badly hurt and needed no treatment, the incident could be repeated and something would need to be done. He talked to the mother about the help which the NSPCC could provide for her, and although she was reluctant at first, in the end she agreed to being visited.

It was clear to the Inspector that this lady was very depressed. Her husband had died the previous year, and she had been coping alone with two small children. Mandy, the younger child, was extremely active and demanding – a lovable child, but quite a handful; her sister Kate, on the other hand, was very subdued and unhappy and had become a frequent bedwetter. These and all the other pressures of recent widowhood built up for the mother, and one evening when she found Kate's bed wet yet again she just snapped and vented her frustration on the older child with a vicious beating. She was very ashamed of herself for having lost control in such a way, and this remorse served only to add to her depression and feeling of being unable to cope.

After a series of visits the mother came to understand that the Society was more concerned with keeping families together than with splitting them up, and she built up the confidence to talk more freely and frankly about her problems. She began to appreciate for herself that Kate's bedwetting was her major source of strain – Mandy's exuberant behaviour and boundless energy were very wearing, but perfectly normal, as many parents will know.

The Inspector arranged a behaviour therapy programme for Kate, who responded very well, and within a few weeks her bedwetting problem had practically disappeared. The girl was very proud of her achievement and seemed happier in herself, and her mother became much more relaxed and was able to be more positive towards her. There were other problems to deal with, but the mother and Kate showed that they were beginning to be more self-reliant in coping with them; in particular the mother took her own initiative in finding a day nursery place for little Mandy, which did them both a power of good, especially when the mother felt able to assist there herself. Before long it became possible to close the case; the changes that had taken place within the family meant that the children were no longer felt to be at serious risk, family relationships were better, the main sources of stress had been coped with and there was a good rapport with their GP. Mother had social contacts outside the home, too, through helping the staff at the nursery.

While both these cases are instances of children being caused unnecessary suffering, manifested in different ways, the important difference is in the outcome. For Sarah (or 'Oi') there was seen to be no hope of achieving any change in her stepfather's outlook or attitude, and the only thing to do for her safety, and for her to have a chance of picking up and leading a normal life, was for her to be removed from home. For Kate and Mandy, on the other hand, although one episode of savage beating could have become repeated and got worse, putting both girls in great danger, their mother had herself come forward to ask for help, and was seen to respond so positively when it was given that vigilance could slowly be eased off and the family helped to stay together in a home that became, as all homes should be, a safe haven for the children.

This choice – between removing the children or keeping the family together with appropriate supervision and support – demonstrates the main dilemma facing those who work with child abuse and neglect, whatever its nature, and more examples will appear in the pages that follow. And in order to understand the issues involved in such cases we need first to look at the nature of child abuse, how widespread it is and the forms it can take.

The Background

Cruelty to children can be traced back through the ages, but for a long time no one gave it a thought. In some religions children were used for human sacrifice, and people as cultured as in the old civilisations of China and of Greece had traditions of unwanted babies being placed outside the city to starve, like fledglings ousted from the nest.

Writing in *Psychology Today* the psycho-historian Lloyd DeMause contributed an article, 'Our Forebears Made Childhood A Nightmare' (April 1975), in which he recorded that 'Virtually every child-rearing tract from antiquity to the eighteenth century recommended the beating of children.' Milton beat his nephews, Beethoven whipped his pupils, John Wesley's babies 'were taught to fear the rod, and to cry softly' – even the infant King Louis XIII of France had a morning beating for his sins of the previous day.

Dickens painted vivid pictures of the suffering of underprivileged little mites, and of their exploitation by the unscrupulous such as Fagin and Bill Sykes. His revelations in his great novels stimulated some of the dedicated Victorian philanthropists, who founded great child-care institutions like Dr Barnado's and set the stage for the creation of the National Society for the Prevention of Cruelty to Children.

There were other actors on the stage. A Mr Agnew of Liverpool, visiting the city of New York, was interested to see an office with the nameplate 'New York Society for the Prevention of Cruelty to Children'. He went inside and heard the tale of their foundation in 1874, and of their subsequent activities; and as soon as he got home he interrupted a meeting convened to discuss animal welfare and protested the need for protection for children. As a result the Liverpool Society for the Prevention of Cruelty to Children was founded – and it nominally exists to this day, although in 1954 it formally became the Liverpool & Birkenhead Branch of the NSPCC.

Mr Agnew's initiative did not pass unnoticed in the metropolis. A number of influential people, including Baroness Burdett-Coutts, took up the cause of cruelty to children, among them a clergyman deeply involved in the plight of the city's young – the Revd Benjamin Waugh. As a result of their efforts there was a meeting at the Mansion House on 7 July 1884, attended by many notables including the well-respected Dr Barnado, and the London Society for the Prevention of Cruelty to Children was born. Waugh was Hon. Secretary, and later became the first Director; branches began to be formed in Hastings, Bristol and elswhere; and in 1889 the name was changed to the National Society for the Prevention of Cruelty to Children. It became incorporated by Royal Charter, which was granted by Queen Victoria in 1895.

The story of how the New York Society began is extra-ordinary. In the USA, as in this country, children had no rights in law at all; they were purely their parents' chattels, entirely at their mercy, and there were neither legal grounds for anyone to intervene in how children were treated nor any acceptance of a duty, let alone a right, to do so. Not everyone felt comfortable about this, and some good souls became increasingly alarmed at the desperate plight of some New York children. But what could they do without legal powers? Then they thought of the legislation to protect animals, and when a particularly celebrated case of child cruelty came to light, involving a girl known as Mary Ellen, the problem was taken to the New York Society for the Prevention of Cruelty to Animals. If children were not citizens, not human beings according to law, since they were alive they must be animals: could the law, they argued, be so interpreted as to help them?

Mr H. Bergh of the NYSPCA did not, despite the legend, prosecute in this way, but he was able to propose how a case might be brought using habeas corpus, and the parents were successfully prosecuted. The public outcry that followed provided the stimulus that was needed, and the NYSPCC was formed, and functions still, as does the Massachusetts Society, which followed shortly afterwards.

A piquant twist to this tale is that some years before, Mr Bergh had passed through London on his way home to New York. He was interested to see an office there with the nameplate 'Royal Society for the Prevention of Cruelty to Animals'. He went inside, and from what he learned determined to set up a similar Society when he reached New York. The wheel completed its full circle when the NSPCC was founded (as the London Society), and was offered accommodation by the RSPCA until it could achieve its own offices.

Was Cruelty Different Then?

There is no doubt that in those nineteenth-century conditions the striking aspects of child cruelty were very different from today. It was calculated that in London alone 2,000 children died each year from 'overlaying' – asphyxiation of the smallest and most feeble in the family as they crowded into their common bed and often drunken parents lay on top of them. Poverty, overcrowding, filth and cold, all took their toll, as did indifference and selfish exploitation. If a parent insured a baby and it chanced to die, at least the survivors might be fed from the insurance. Baby farming was rife, with such cynical disregard for the lives of the unwanted children that Societies already existed in France, Spain and elsewhere in Europe, which bore the titles 'For the Prevention of Cruelty to Children' but were in fact set up specifically to challenge this particular evil.

Benjamin Waugh was keen to point out the wider remit over here. Wilful cruelty, neglect and sexual exploitation, of whatever nature and wherever they occurred across society, were all the subject of NSPCC activity, and in 1887 he wrote in *The Child's Guardian*:

> We are informed by a correspondent that France has a Society like the London Society. Our reply is that our correspondent is mistaken: France has no such society as the London Society. Our friends in France should know this and try to alter it. There is a society known as 'The Society for the Protection of Children', whose office is at 4 Rue des Beaux Arts, it was founded in 1865, and recognised by decree in 1869. But its origin was in view of the craze of Frenchmen against population, a craze which has taken root and is growing amongst us . . . It has succeeded in its limited aims, which are stated as follows:
>
> To diminish baby mortality by
>
> 1. Encouraging nursing by mothers.
> 2. Improving the character and condition of nurses.
> 3. Spreading a better knowledge of child treatment.
> 4. Protecting from ill usage.
>
> This last object, which is the mainstay of our work, appears in France to have been an afterthought, and there does not seem to have been the means or time to act upon it.

It is interesting that while the Society had been founded during the times of great Christian philanthropic enterprise, its founders recognised that its workers should be acceptable in any community, in any home, and wrote firmly out of its constitution any provision for Christian let alone denominational bias. The Chief Rabbi joined with the Archbishop of Canterbury and the Cardinal Archbishop of Westminster as patrons, and their successors hold such titles still.

This is not a book about the NSPCC, and there is not space to trace the development of its caseload through the decades. Since those early days the rank outright poverty has gone; the mortality rates for infants and children have dropped; the arbitrary and authoritarian response to cases has evolved into a more professional and structured involvement; and there has grown a realisation of the greater complexity and range of child abuse. Life is more complex today and there is a much wider range and number of professional agencies involved, but cruelty and deprivation still exist, and a more affluent society has not yet learned to cope. It is probable that many of the cases being dealt with nowadays would have been seen as too minor for attention when so much was life-threatening in the past, and while I do not have the facts to support this statement, it is my feeling that nowadays we are dealing at a more preventive stage with many cases of physical injury and neglect; nevertheless, extreme examples of gross and wilful cruelty still occur, and our knowledge of the degree of sexual assault and injury is limited and recent. Human nature does not alter much, and cruel acts and murderous intent have been with us since Cain murdered Abel.

How Do You Define Abuse?

Reports of desperate tragedies in foreign lands – flood, famine or man-made disaster – produce instant reactions of horror and sympathy among the British public. Tales of cruelty to animals in our own land produce a similar response. But although the position is changing, there is understandably a different reaction to child abuse. Cruelty to *children*, in our own land? In our own *street*? This is more difficult to stomach, and even when we overcome our initial rejection of the idea we are unable to comprehend just how widespread the needless suffering of children really is across our society, let alone to accept the different forms it can take.

Definitions do not necessarily help our understanding, and the fact that there are many only shows that none is adequate. But if we say that

> child abuse occurs when any avoidable act, or avoidable failure to act, adversely affects the physical, mental or emotional well-being of a child,

and if we think of this in the context of the abuser normally being a parent or other person responsible for the child's care, we have an overall description which we can use as a beginning.

What is 'an avoidable act'? It is important to note that this means something that happened, which need not have happened, but which also need not have been deliberate. If a child is struck, with a fist, or a belt or a length of wire, that is an avoidable act – and it is also deliberate. If an angry parent picks up and shakes an erring child, and unintentionally causes a brain haemorrhage which can kill or permanently disable, that is just as much an avoidable act; that it was not deliberate cruelty does not lessen the cruelty of the outcome, although it may well affect what action is taken to protect the child (or others in the family) from further abuse.

It is avoidable acts that we usually think of when we mention child abuse; and it is also physical acts that come to mind. If we think about it a little more, it is obvious that cruel or unfeeling physical hurt may well have psychological implications too – the cowed, pale and listless child who suffers constant bullying may lose the self-confidence, the very incentive, to grow emotionally or intellectually to anything like her potential. But this hidden injury – what I call 'the invisible scarring', which may never show on X-ray but is just as real as any physical hurt, and often longer lasting – may come from other avoidable acts than blows, or burns, or shaking. How many of us remember the crushing sarcasm of a relative, or schoolteacher, which was often feared far more than physical punishment, or the penetrating cruelty of jibes, perhaps from other children, at some weakness or physical deformity? Indeed, emotional abuse can take many forms, as we shall see in Chapter 7, and it can be deliberately inflicted; sometimes it may be due to apathy or lack of understanding of a child's need to be valued and encouraged, sometimes it can be the effect of parents putting their own ambitions and priorities before the needs of their child.

It is perhaps more difficult to grasp that failure to act can also be cruelty. Yet children can die of neglect, and thousands have blighted or less than adequate lives – with all too much likelihood of passing their experience on to the next generation. Fig. 1 shows that in any one year the NSPCC may deal with more referrals of neglect than almost all other categories put together.

Neglect – the failure to provide for, or to protect a child – can also be a deliberate act: withholding food beyond all

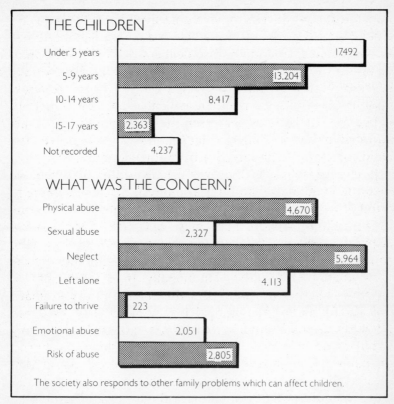

THE CHILDREN

Under 5 years	17,492
5-9 years	13,204
10-14 years	8,417
15-17 years	2,363
Not recorded	4,237

WHAT WAS THE CONCERN?

Physical abuse	4,670
Sexual abuse	2,327
Neglect	5,964
Left alone	4,113
Failure to thrive	223
Emotional abuse	2,051
Risk of abuse	2,805

The society also responds to other family problems which can affect children.

FIG. 1. REFERRALS FOR ABUSE
1 OCTOBER 1986–30 SEPTEMBER 1987

reason as 'punishment' for some trivial 'offence'; delaying going to the doctor in the hope that a baby's condition will get worse – 'She'll have to go to hospital now, won't she, Doc?' is something a mother has said to me more than once when I was a GP.

More often neglect is the sad consequence of ignorance and apathy: the squawling baby with raw infected skin from being left in sodden filthy nappies; the puny child sucking hungrily at a bottle containing weak tea instead of a decent feed; the constant onset of illness and infection that can unnecessarily threaten life for some poor child who is undernourished, underclothed and living in squalid filth. There can also be neglect to protect children from outside dangers or domestic hazards that they are too young to understand or cope with.

Many new mothers fret unnecessarily when their first baby cries, until they come to recognise (sometimes with granny to help) whether baby is hungry, ill or just letting off steam. There are others who do not know, and cannot bring themselves to care, when their child is in distress and urgently needs attention.

Again, neglect need not only refer to physical needs for warmth and food and the opportunity to stretch one's limbs and learn to use them. A child's mind and spirit also need to be stretched and helped to develop. Most of all, a child needs to be *loved*, and failure to provide a child with love is the saddest of all 'avoidable failures' to provide for a child's well-being. To those who have had a loving home, it can be hard to understand the hopelessness of existence within some households (one cannot call them homes) or to appreciate how easily two young people may try to escape from similar backgrounds through the time-honoured route of pregnancy, and then look to their new baby to give them the love they have never had. It can't. It therefore is rejected, and the cycle of deprivation moves on one generation more.

How Much Abuse is There?

We have established that cruelty to children can take many forms, and that it can affect body, mind, or spirit; and have realised that cruelty can come from wilful actions, or mistaken ones – and that it can also result from failing to provide for a child's physical or mental needs, or from failure to protect. Now we must look at the scale of the problem and how many children are affected.

As I will discuss in the next chapter, there is as yet no national record of child abuse statistics, although there are at last signs of movement. This makes it difficult to assess the true extent of the problem. In this book I shall be referring to two sets of data – the NSPCC's own cases, and the NSPCC Register Research.

NSPCC Casework Statistics
For over a century the NSPCC has kept records of the

numbers of cases in different categories that have come to its attention; indeed in its early years these figures were updated in every issue of the Society's newspaper *The Child's Guardian*. In recent years these figures have appeared regularly in the Annual Report, and the latest figures are shown in Fig. 2.

Referrals and Cases	
Referrals* received in year	23,175
Children involved	45,713
Children in open cases 1.10.86	4,916
Children in open cases 30.9.87	5,217
Children helped in 1986/7	50,629

* Referrals include reports of suspected incidents of child abuse and other concern received by the NSPCC which may require investigation or other assistance.

FIG. 2. THE NSPCC'S WORK IN ENGLAND, WALES AND NORTHERN IRELAND 1 OCTOBER 1986–30 SEPTEMBER 1987

The number of new cases shown for the year, 23,175, and the number of children involved should not be misunderstood as showing necessarily an indicator of incidence of child abuse: what they represent is the number of cases reported to the Society, alleging or confessing to abuse or neglect, and the numbers of children in the households involved. They are the numbers of cases that the Society has had to investigate, and the numbers of children about whom it was necessary to check for their safety, rather than the actual number of proven incidents. In much the same way a fire brigade may log the number of times they have been called out, whether or not there was a fire when they got there. In each case it is a measure of response to calls, rather than a record of findings.

In fact it may often be that the apprehensions voiced by a relative or neighbour, or even the problems mentioned by an anxious parent, are not specifically borne out by the findings when the case is looked into. In a large number of cases what will be found is some degree of disorder or family problem, needing some sort of help, even if the informant was incorrect as to detail. The information that 'Johnny at No 10 is badly bruised – his father's been beating him again' may be found to mean, on enquiry, that Johnny is indeed bruised, but that there is a valid explanation for it; what may also be revealed is that Johnny is a very unhappy child in a family which has bad financial worries and child-rearing problems. Sometimes the whole incident has a perfectly natural explanation, and the informant has misunderstood the position, but it is better to have a call too many than one too few. Rarely, but occasionally, a call may be deliberately malicious, and this is wicked; if one is in the business of protecting children, however, it is a foolish worker who fails to check on the safety of children because of a hunch that a call is bogus – it might not be.

Misleading calls can also be made by parents. It is not unknown for an anonymous call to come in to an NSPCC office, but when a visit is made for the mother to deny any problem – then after repeated anonymous calls it becomes apparent that the mother was in fact the caller. This sort of situation could have happened in the case of the girl called 'Oi!' – a mother too frightened of her husband to take action openly, even putting up a front of resisting enquiries, but hoping against hope for her child's sake that someone will understand the hidden distress signals and work out what is happening.

A variant of this is in the plea for help in some minor way. One mother rang to say that she had no bedclothes for her new baby's cot – could the NSPCC please help? This might hardly seem to be a crisis calling for a skilled child abuse specialist, but you never know – and you need to keep your wits about you. An Inspector called on the mother and produced sheets and blankets; but training tells, and it was natural for him to say, 'While I'm here I might as well have a look at your baby.' Baby was bruised in a way that was not consistent with any natural injuries. Mother had not told on her husband – she was terrified of him – but she had found a way of ensuring her baby's safety.

What is noteworthy from Fig. 3 is that well over 18 per cent of cases were referred by the parents themselves. Adding in referrals from other relatives this means that 29 per cent of cases came to the Society from members of the family, compared with 58 per cent from the general public. The monsters who deal cruelly with children out of deliberate malice are deservedly condemned; but there are many, many cases where one or both parents are as concerned as anybody that things are working out wrongly; they feel caught up themselves in crises they do not understand; they are aware that they are taking things out on the children, although they do not want to – and cannot understand why they do. 'Please help me!' begged one distraught young mother down the telephone. 'I've locked my little girl in her bedroom, because if I get near her I'll do something desperate to her! Help me!'

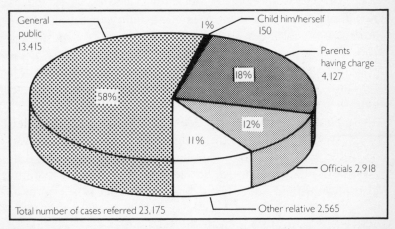

General public 13,415

Child him/herself 150

1%

Parents having charge 4,127

18%

58%

12%

11%

Officials 2,918

Total number of cases referred 23,175

Other relative 2,565

FIG.3 WHO TOLD THE NSPCC? 1 OCTOBER 1986–30 SEPTEMBER 1987

Sometimes what might be suspected as a child abuse injury has a perfectly natural explanation, but compared with the overall number of cases dealt with, the proportion is pretty small. It is not pleasant to feel that you are being suspected of injuring your own children, when there is nothing the matter, but that should never deter parents from taking their children for medical attention whenever they need it. If somebody dies suddenly, and they have not seen a doctor recently, the coroner needs to be informed, the coroner's officer will need to make some routine enquiries and there may have to be a post mortem examination, even perhaps an inquest. When there has been nothing criminal or negligent happen to cause that death, the family might well wish that such enquiries did not have to be made – but they know that they should. The same acceptance should apply when a child is injured.

We have moved on from the days when parents had absolute rights and children had none. If we accept that child abuse is wrong, and can be a criminal offence, then we should surely also accept that whenever a child is injured some responsible person, such as the doctor in Casualty, has a duty to bear in mind that not every injury is accidental, and to ask the appropriate questions, and, like the coroner's officer, to do so tactfully, but steadfastly.

A colleague told me of a young lad who started at a new school. He had not been there very long when the headmaster asked to see both parents. When they came for their appointment, the head seemed a bit tense as he asked them if everything was all right at home. The father quickly realised the position, and said, 'Don't you worry! Our youngster's puffy face and tear-stained cheeks are due to terrible hay fever. However, you were quite right to ask to see us, and I'm especially glad that you were alert enough to consider that there might be a child abuse problem, and felt that you ought to do something about it. I say "especially" because you may not know that I am Child Abuse Consultant with the NSPCC.'

Cases of non-accidental injury, or baby battering, as it came to be nicknamed for a while, figure prominently – especially when you add the number of cases where there was serious concern over children being at risk. Most people think of child abuse in terms of physical injury – indeed, until Henry Kempe coined the phrase 'the battered baby syndrome' in 1962 the popular concept was of bullying or of over-zealous beating of older children. Certainly it is the most easily recognised, the best researched – and the most often fatal – form of cruelty. However, when you look at the cases of neglect, and add the specific type of neglect known as leaving alone, these jointly come to over 40 per cent of the total. The next highest figure relates to cases where there were emotional problems; emotional abuse is indeed widespread, very varied in nature, and often difficult to pinpoint.

When we seek to establish the real incidence of child abuse in this country, it is important to understand that the number of cases being referred to the NSPCC does not necessarily relate to the overall total, because, due to inconsistencies in the way cases are recorded, no one knows how many cases are seen by the 120 or so Social Services Departments in England, Wales and Nothern Ireland[1]. Fig. 2 on p. 15 shows the cases taken by the NSPCC in 1987, and all that I can say with certainty is that this represents the work undertaken by the NSPCC during that year.

NSPCC Register Research
The Register Research figures are probably more representative than any others of the true state of suspected and proven cases of abuse. The NSPCC acts as agent for a number of local authorities by managing their child abuse registration systems. The areas covered contain just under 10 per cent of the child population of England and Wales. Multiply these figures by just over ten, and you should have a fair estimate of the national incidence of cases which have been detected and established as abuse. The figures in Fig. 4 are based on a more scientific approach. We can have some idea of the scale of the problem if we assume that at the end of 1987 there were about 54,000 children named on child abuse registers, about 25,600 of whom were new cases during that year. We will have to return to the conundrum of how far these figures represent the true state of childhood suffering; first let us look at why that suffering happens, whether it is getting worse and in more detail at what forms that suffering can take.

	1987
Estimated number of children aged 0–14 physically abused in England & Wales	8044
Estimated number of children aged 0–16 sexually abused in England & Wales	7119

FIG.4 ESTIMATED NUMBERS OF ABUSED CHILDREN
1 OCTOBER 1986–30 SEPTEMBER 1987

[1] The law, and child abuse procedures, are different in Scotland, but the RSSPCC reports comparable incidence figures.

Chapter Two: **Why Does Abuse Happen?**

'Who could possibly do such a thing?' is a common reaction whenever a case of child abuse comes to public notice. And if one tries to explain that so many offenders against their children are often as much victims as those they injure, many will say, 'How can you condone such monsters?' This is a reaction that I can understand; what makes me uneasy is the person who carries on by saying, 'I've brought up a family and we have never had any problems between us.'

Frankly, I do not believe such an assertion; and if the person who makes it believes it to be true, then I fear for the true state of that family. Who among us does not remember as a child having moments of rage or outright rebellion against a parent or other grown-up? What parent does not recall some episode of tension and perhaps downright unfairness in reacting to a child? It is a natural thing to have moments of conflict within a family, as a growing child tries to develop independence, or test out the limits of parental tolerance. It is inevitable that mistakes will be made, and there can be few of us as parents who do not recall an episode when we wish that we had been firmer in refusing a child's request, for his or her own good; more often, perhaps, we have a shameful recollection of being unreasonable and unnecessarily crushing – probably because we were preoccupied with something else and did not want to be bothered.

Such incidents are part of the normal range of human reactions, and when the underlying relationship is a loving and caring one there is seldom lasting hurt. The difficulty comes when normal reactions reach abnormal proportions, or when there is no capacity for love or proper understanding – and this poverty of spirit is no respecter of social class or material wealth.

It is true that there are monsters: people who will cold-bloodedly torture some helpless innocent and take perverted pleasure in the suffering they cause. There may well be an added sadism in inflicting pain and misery upon some little tot who is too puny to try any form of defence – the more an infant cowers, the more placidly a tiny baby lies there and takes it (what else can it do?) the greater the urge to hurt, and hurt again.

But while such pathological torturers, who may develop into brutal killers, undoubtedly exist (and when they are identified they need to be removed from a society that cannot cope with them), they are relatively few, and the cases of child abuse and neglect are, as we have seen, counted in their tens of thousands. Why is this?

If there were a clear answer to this question life would be a lot easier, because one would be able to focus preventive actions upon an identifiable group and really come to grips with protecting those children who are at risk. One of our current troubles is that we are able to define 'at-risk groups' only in such broad general terms as to be of little use; so many families come into such a category that it would take an army of child-care staff to monitor them all. Protective removal of all such children into care would be an unthinkable exercise – and harm far more children than were helped; the days of the great Victorian orphanages would be a golden age of enlighten-ment compared with having tens or even hundreds of thousands of children taken from their homes into protective care.

For example, some would say that one should take especial care of stepchildren. Cinderella was not the only stepchild to suffer rejection and other forms of emotional and physical abuse. It is a favourite stereotype to picture the new husband, anxious to father his own children, who rejects and cruelly treats his wife's children from a previous marriage. Heidi Koseda died in such circumstances, as did Kimberley Carlile, and others. But it would be monstrous to suggest that all stepchildren are at special risk and (if it were feasible to find people to do it) should have special surveillance. Step-parents who abuse are not typical, but people with problems of their own. Nearly every stepfather or mother is very aware of the need to build up a special bond with their partner's children and is committed to loving them; they are more likely to be over-sensitive than insensitive to the challenges of being accepted as a substitute parent.

There are many other characteristics of child abuse which we can identify and try to make into a pattern. The danger is in trying to make that pattern fit the theory of the moment, rather than place it in perspective. It is so tempting to put forward a glib explanation that means that the problem can be filed away without further effort — like the editor of my one-time local newspaper, who once wrote to say that there was no need to spend any time analysing the problem of child abuse — it was all quite simply due to 'parents who lacked moral fibre'. What sort of diet would put that right was not disclosed. For caring people, the issue of why child abuse happens is one that cannot be ducked in such a facile way, and when we are dealing with complex disturbances in human behaviour that means undertaking a long period of painstaking observation and fact-finding.

Is It The Children?

One example of this research lies in the analysis which has taken place for years within the NSPCC as its statistics are collected and collated. 'What are the characteristics of the child?' we ask. One could identify many. If children are being abused, and if sometimes only one child in a large family was affected, are there characteristics in the children that might be the precipitating cause?

One obvious candidate for abuse is the child who is hyperactive — bounding with energy and curiosity, appearing to exist without sleep, always demanding, always into scrapes — a candidate for increasingly tired and short-tempered parents to lash out at. How many of us, as parents, have said at one time or another, 'If you don't stop these constant questions I'll wring your little neck!'? Few of us have meant it, of course.

In labelling a child as 'hyperactive' – or any other category – there can be scope for being dangerously slipshod. A lazy or unsympathetic parent, faced with the demands of a perfectly normal, healthy, energetic child, can dismiss his inability (or lack of inclination) to cope with his child as being the child's fault – 'She is hyperactive, of course', or 'She is disturbed, and won't respond whatever care I give her.' This is not to suggest for one moment that hyperactivity is not a very real problem, on which interesting work is being done by looking at dietary factors and the effect of certain food additives. But I am trying to point out the risk of glib use of a convenient label. The 'underactive' parent can label the child 'hyperactive'; the disturbed parent can say it is the child that is disturbed. The child so labelled takes the responsibility for the problem in the eyes of the parent, who can come to believe that this is so – and resent the child for it; and the child, feeling resented and rejected, can then begin to become disturbed in consequence.

We know also that children with low birthweights are abused more often than we would expect. This could be due to the frequent need for special care, which would result in separation, impeding the attachment process between parent and child.

Or there's the crying baby: so often the story begins with, 'It was the crying that did it!' – a fraught mother with an uncaring husband, too many children, and the baby cries, and cries, and cries. One such mother, when her nerves were frayed beyond endurance, placed the baby in its carry cot outside her bedroom window on a little balcony. She gained a few hours' sleep, oblivious to the snow that began to fall until her child was dead. She was no monster: she just couldn't cope and there was no one to help her.

It is not always the mother who is strained by crying. Mary McDell was taken to a London clinic by her mother. Mary, aged nine months, was one of four children who had always been well cared for, being neatly dressed, well fed and having had regular clinic checkups. Mrs McDell had seemed in many ways to be the ideal housewife and mother and her case was therefore surprising to clinic staff.

Mary had bruising to face and arms, fingermarks being clearly visible. It seemed that the child had been distressed throughout the night and had disturbed both her parents. In the morning Mrs McDell had slept on whilst her husband had got Mary up and dressed. When in due course Mrs McDell awoke and realised that something had happened to the child she dressed the other children – twins aged five and an older daughter aged seven – and took them to a neighbour's house whilst she visited the clinic.

In the investigation that followed the story emerged of a number of dissatisfactions within the marriage relating to the management of money and the roles within the home, and little Mary's restless night had been the final straw for Mr McDell in a long series of minor frustrations and irritations. Each time Mary cried Mr McDell woke up. Three times Mrs McDell went and settled her. Father, half asleep, irritable, perhaps feeling helpless, had gone to prepare breakfast for the children and finally lashed out at Mary. He had expressed considerable remorse at the time and since and at no time attempted to deny his actions. Mr McDell in fact was quite bewildered at finding himself capable of such an act.

Much work followed with this family, including helping the parents to look at their own relationship and the way they divided up their responsibilities and also how they managed the care of the various children.

A year later this family had become the nice family that everyone had thought them to be and workers were confident enough to suggest that Mary's name be removed from the Child Abuse Register, having been placed there at the time of the original injury.

Then there is the scapegoat: the awkward one in the family, the 'ugly duckling', for some reason of a different physical or mental make-up who gets picked on when anything goes wrong. The unwanted child, who appears because of an unexpected pregnancy, or as the result of an extra-marital affair, or who is a constant reminder of a difficult labour or an unhappy ante-natal period, may have almost an 'inherited' stigma which makes scapegoating very likely.

The other children soon find out that their road to safety from parental wrath is to point the finger at the unpopular brother – or provoke him into an act which can make him seem to be the transgressor. Their motives can be mixed: diverting aggression upon someone who will suffer anyway, in an instinct for self-preservation; seeking, Judas-like, their reward.

The child who is different, like one with a handicap or deformity, can often become a particular focus for maternal attention as if to compensate – indeed the rest of the family may suffer deprivation. That great and compassionate paediatrician, the late Sir Wilfrid Sheldon, often advised parents of a Down's Syndrome ('mongol') child to have it placed in residential care, not because of any doubt as to the care it would be given: on the contrary, his concern was that the other children in the family could be neglected while mother instinctively devoted herself to protecting her most vulnerable nestling. But other unwanted children are resented and made to suffer for their presence – as though they could help it.

There are those, too, who seem to court parental anger – the trouble-seekers. If there is a way of making father angry, of getting into mother's way at the wrong time, and being made to suffer for it – there they will be. It is as if there were some masochistic drive to be the target for anger and for angry blows. That is exactly what can happen, of course, and when we were young most of us saw an example of it among our contemporaries. To be deliberately naughty, to make a grown-up angry, may be the only way some child can be noticed; punishment may be excessive, suffering may be great, but at least you have been the focus of someone's attention; at least you have mattered enough for someone to be angry with you and hit you – being totally rejected and ignored can be even worse.

Such behaviour can also result from other disturbances. The child who is being sexually abused, or damaged and humiliated in other ways, can have all sorts of mixed feelings of anger and shame and resentment. This can affect behaviour in various ways, one of which is by angry and aggressive behaviour directed at adults, despite the consequences – or against other children. This can lead him or her into even greater trouble.

It need not always be deliberate abuse that leads to abuse-provoking behaviour by active children. I was once at a church meeting in south London, when a new minister was confronted with a demand for action to get better police protection for the church, which was being soiled and vandalised by local children. To his credit, new as he was, he challenged the request. 'Why do we need the police?' he asked. 'In what way are we as a community failing these children that they behave like this?' This jolted his audience into a different attitude and discussion centred upon the observation that many children were turfed out of their homes because their play disturbed adult enjoyment of the ubiquitous television. Small wonder that they felt resentful and rejected, and showed their feelings. Instead of a police alarm the church decided to seek Lambeth Council's help in employing a youth worker and creating a centre in the church that would be open every day to give the children a place they would be welcome and activities which would use their energies less harmfully. This was some compensation for the minor but persistent abuse that they were experiencing in the form of rejection and neglect.

A totally different concept is provided by the idealised child. Parents may have such high ideals, such unrealistic expectations of what their child can achieve, that the child is a constant disappointment when it fails, as it is bound to, for their ideals are impossible. The young couple, attracted to each other partly at least because they both want to escape from an unhappy and over-rigid home, produce a baby and look towards its coming through rose-tinted spectacles. Here is someone at last, their very own baby, who will give them the love and comfort they have never known. It cannot do so, poor little mite; it needs love and comfort that they do not know how to give. It is then rejected as a disappointment; the cycle of emotional deprivation moves on one generation, followed perhaps by neglect, and even physical injury.

In a different way perfectionist parents, perhaps with a professional background, can have an idealised concept of their child achieving standards of behaviour that reflect their own adult outlook; they do not see that a child is a child and not a mini-adult. If they have done well at school and in higher education, they look to their child to achieve their own ambitions and to outshine all others, when this might be a totally unrealistic appraisal of that child's capabilities. The stresses and agonies such a child can go through, trying to live up to an unattainable ideal, can be very disabling; yet the parents would be upset to be told that they are trying to fulfil themselves, rather than their child – at the expense of his or her happiness.

I was once asked to advise about a lad who was a young terror in his behaviour, and whose chances of a good career seemed to be doomed by inexplicably poor performance in exams. When I met him he was a pleasant youngster, with a good personality, considerable initiative and inventiveness, and highly intelligent. What was wrong? His parents were both exceptionally able people – both professors in fact – and they both placed too high a value on their expectations of his academic performance, and too little on his need for affection, understanding and encouragement. He reacted against this by using his powers of leadership and creativeness in destructive ways, ways that were destructive too of his own prospects. He was always fearful of failing to match up to parental expectations academically, and so he deliberately neglected his studies and perversely went out of his way to fail examinations, because he could not be sure that he would do well enough and come top every time. With a bit of support, he had the strength of character to pull himself out of his rut and do what he had always longed to – achieve well in a professional career. But the sad thing was that had he had a proper upbringing, he would have been brilliant enough to have outshone both his parents.

Or Is It the Parents?

While these observations are true, they do not explain why

abuse happens to children who do not seem to have any special characteristics. What is even more perplexing is that if hyperactivity, say, or an unwanted pregnancy, are causative factors in child abuse, why are only some children in such categories the victims of abuse? Many cases of abuse occur when certain parents just cannot cope with the behaviour, or even the basic needs, of perfectly normal children. Could it be that there are particular characteristics of the parents in such cases?

All sorts of analyses have taken place about parents who abuse their children. Research shows that children who are neglected or abused live in less stable families than non-abused children. In 1987 only 38 per cent of physically abused children were living with both natural parents when abuse occurred; this figure was higher in cases of emotional abuse, and lower in sexual abuse and much lower in cases of neglect. Over a quarter of children placed on child abuse registers in the NSPCC series were living with their mothers and a stepfather or 'uncle', and just under a quarter with their mothers alone; this applied particularly to neglected children.

Statistical findings need to be looked at with very great care, so as to avoid glib assumptions that may be wrong. For example, in a series of cases recorded over the five-year period from 1977 to 1982, the NSPCC found that 1,230 children had been physically injured by their own ('natural') mothers and 1,249 had been injured by their natural fathers. This would seem to give the impression that mothers and fathers are equally likely to be the perpetrators of physical abuse; but this isn't true. Many more of these children are living with their natural mothers than with their natural fathers, so you would expect many more children to be abused by their mothers if that assumption was correct. Taking these factors into account, we get the figures that fathers were instrumental in 60 per cent of the physical injury cases when they were with their children, and mothers in 36 per cent. (To take this matter further would be beyond the scope of this book, and readers who are interested in more detail should contact the NSPCC Librarian in the first instance.)

Immaturity of parents is another factor which seems to be fairly consistent, although this varies with different types of abuse. Overall, mothers who were under twenty years old at the time of the birth of the child who was subsequently abused appear in the research samples three times more often than would be expected. The sexually abused children's mothers were also younger, appearing twice as often as would be expected, although they and the sexually abused children were older when the abuse was ascertained.

Maturity does not of course relate solely to calendar age. Some abusing fathers may have moved on in years but still have an adolescent aggressiveness, anti-social behaviour and an immature need to assert themselves which can underlie the way that they respond to their children and their wives.

For some years the NSPCC maintained a small research unit into marital violence – nicknamed the 'Yo-Yo Unit' because it was apparent that children's fortunes went up and down like a yo-yo according to the state of warfare or truce between the parents. It observed that children can suffer in a variety of ways. The tension, anger, emotional conflict and physical aggression between parents all have an effect, even upon children thought too young to comprehend, which can be deeply disturbing and leave long-term scars. In the course of marital conflict children may be physically attacked in either separate or parallel violence. They may be rejected or struck because they are evidence of their mother's (or father's) existence; or they may be attacked as an oblique way of getting at their rejected spouse. They may receive injury incidentally to the spouse being attacked, for instance when the child a mother is nursing or protecting is hurt when she is knocked down. There are many instances of touching heroism when some small child will try to defend his or her mother and stand between her and the attacking father or stepfather. Withdrawn or troublesome children at school can be reflecting, in unusual and anti-social behaviour, how wounded and upset they are by their parents' warfare.

Sometimes the family may intervene to help the child – grandparents take them away for a while so that parents can sort themselves out; good for them – but oscillating to and from home can be unsettling in itself, especially when the child is aware that something is wrong and feels excluded from where he or she feels entitled to be and from what he or she feels entitled to know.

Much of this behaviour in adults can be traced back of course to their experience as children. Many cases of abuse and neglect are due to parents who have suffered in their turn – a pattern of behaviour that has been traced back through four or five generations; however, it is important to note that many who have been abused or neglected as children will go to almost any length to protect their own children from any such experience. I can remember a patient of mine telling me that he had been a 'latch-key child' – coming home daily from school to an empty house with the key on a string around his neck so that he could let himself in – and that he was determined, whatever the cost to himself in working extra hours, to earn enough money to have his wife free to be at home because he wanted there always to be someone in when his children came home.

Amongst the parents who abuse and neglect their children there is a range of personality types, at one end of which we find psychopaths. Psychopathic parents may show some of the features of the immature and anti-social parents, being irresponsible, hostile and impulsive, but, more than this, they appear to be totally self-centred, pursuing their own pleasures, obsessions and needs with an indifference to the needs of others, even their own children. If they feel a destructive impulse towards the child, however young, they are capable of the most violent acts. They are not rational and may be the most plausible liars. Their irrationality may mean that they are punitive in their attitude to very young children, inappropriately attributing to them quite adult motivations. To work with the psychopath is most difficult and potentially dangerous for any children involved. Fortunately, as I have said earlier, such individuals are exceptions; we need to identify them as early as possible and deal with them firmly, recognising the dangers that may exist if we fail.

Is It the Relationship?

In looking at why child abuse happens I have tried to look at the features of various participants, the parents and the children that we discover as victims of abuse and neglect. What of course also needs to be said is that it is the relationship – one to another – of husbands and wives, mothers and fathers with their children which add a dynamic to family interactions.

Sometimes a baby is rejected by its parents when the normal process called 'bonding' – the process of an emotional link forming between a mother and her child which begins when the new-born babe is first placed in her arms – is interrupted, particularly when raw young parents have problems. The existence of this bonding process, the development of a deeply satisfying emotional attachment between a mother and her babe, seems so natural and instinctive that it is understandable that it was for so long regarded as something to be taken for granted, rather than as a precious and essential ingredient in developing a relationship which needed, like all relationships, to be given the right climate for taking root and growing.

Men can never fully comprehend, because they cannot experience, the emotional as well as the physical impact of carrying a child, of labouring to give it birth, of hearing its cry as it takes its first breath of independent existence; but they should be aware of its significance and, as fathers, should whenever possible share in and support those precious early acts of bonding when their child is born. The act of placing a new-born baby in its mother's arms physically aids the completion of labour, and emotionally is a time of awe and wonderment. Or so it should be, as mother responds to baby learning to have the warmth and comfort and security of being in her arms, to gaze at and learn to focus on her face, to reach out and learn to feel, to nuzzle against her for nourishment.

The ideal is not always achievable; birth may not be natural, breast-feeding may not work or there can be other interruptions. The baby may not have been wanted; labour may have been difficult; the baby may have imperfections;

there can be reasons why it is, or becomes, resented or rejected, which all the natural opportunities for fulfilment may not always overcome. As I write, there is news of women who have abortions to rid them of unwanted female foetuses, for there are cultures where bearing unwanted girls is a stigma; dynasties too, although even his contemporaries thought that King Henry VIII went too far in his attempts to ensure a male heir.

Whatever the reasons, if the natural bonding between mother and child is diminished or is absent, then that child can be greatly at risk, and those involved in caring must be alert to this, the midwife most of all. I remember working in an obstetric ward where a young mother pushed her new-born baby to one side and looked down at her own body – 'Am I torn?' was all that she wanted to know. The danger to that child can come from its mother's own actions, or inaction; or, because she is heedless to its well-being, because she does not protect it from cruelty by her partner, or by others, since the normal fierce protectiveness of a mother for her young is missing. It is now recognised as being important that separation of mother and child even for good professional reasons threatens their relationship and must be either avoided, or modified as much as possible and steps taken to compensate.

Professional people are more alert to this problem now, but in my medical student days I remember the dismay with which we greeted the news that a premature baby with extensive abnormalities, which had been cured by miracles of surgical and anaesthetic skill, was rejected and eventually left to die by his immature young parents. What no one had allowed for, because in those days it was not thought about, was the feelings of a very immature mother whose baby had appeared unexpectedly early, when she was not prepared for it (and had not even wanted it), only to have it whisked away to an incubator in a special premature baby unit, then to the operating theatre and a surgical ward, then to intensive care, until weeks later she was given what was by then an unwelcome stranger with a large surgical scar – and was told how lucky she was. While understanding has grown, there can still be circumstances, where illness or other adversity can thwart successful bonding between mother and new-born child. Nevertheless much is being done in special-care practice to help this problem, such as allowing parents to stay with their hospitalised baby, to have a photograph to have with them when they go home, and to have counselling care which helps them to think about their baby, prepare themselves for its needs, identify with it and feel involved in what is being done.

The significance of the relationship between parent and child which is formed through bonding has been increasingly recognised. In 1983 the NSPCC changed the focus of their research and asked questions which enquired about the characteristics of relationships in the family. Two of the new factors most frequently quoted were the inability to respond to the emotional needs of the child and the inability to deal with normal child behaviour. Research shows that abused and neglected children do not emerge as significantly more handicapped or difficult than other children. Parents more often fail to deal with the normal developing child than with gross child disturbance. In looking for causes we see that there can be a number of possible trigger factors, like the behaviour of a particular child, or the circumstances in which a family lives, which may contribute to the abuse of children but do not explain it, because thousands of other households meet the same circumstances.

Debt and unemployment can exacerbate the pressure on the family especially when the adults in it had unstable, unsatisfying and stressful relationships, all leading to a crisis point when child abuse might occur. What does become clear is that this is a very complex matter when we try to assess the detail, but that the basic failing is that some parents are unable to manage their children, and may be unable to control themselves when dealing with their children. All parents can understand the stresses, many can identify with particular strains or difficulties, but few can accept how or why children should be made to suffer.

Chapter Three: **Is It Getting Worse?**

'Child abuse figures soar!' say the banner headlines. 'This is the worst case there has ever been,' says the judge. 'These social workers don't know what they are doing!' say the armchair critics. The ordinary caring person hearing these begins to wonder if sanity, and law and order, have taken flight and child cruelty is on the rampage. It is so easy to make sweeping statements; so tempting to sit back and make harsh criticisms of what others are (allegedly) failing to do – but so much harm can result.

The temptation to make complacent statements and high-sounding generalisations is one to be resisted. They may be reassuring to the person who makes them, and indeed to those of his audience who would prefer such issues just to go away, but they may not be helpful to the children. We are definitely in an area where there are fragments of the truth in almost any assertion that is made – but where also there is a great risk of distortion. The difficulty in assessing and working with child abuse is in finding a true balance of the facts, when knowledge is imperfect and the variable factors are almost infinite; and the task is all the more difficult because we are dealing with explaining, understanding – and, above all, trying to predict – how individual human beings may act in circumstances of which we have only partial, and possibly misleading, knowledge.

The first point to be clear about is what we mean by increases. We must ask if there is more abuse of children these days – or whether we are more aware of its existence and therefore discovering more cases that were really there all the time? If the very concept of parents sexually violating their own children was unthinkable, and therefore unacceptable, until quite recently, does that mean that it did not happen before? Or were there children who were suffering in silence because no one would listen to them or believe them if they did try to get help?

For example, in the case of sexual abuse, there is no doubt whatsoever that for generations, right up until the 1980s, the disbelief that any such events could happen in apparently normal homes led to absolute rejection of any evidence to the contrary. It was so unbelievable that there was a sort of mental block, or subconscious wilful blindness, that meant that children had no hope of relief. Yet there is ample evidence that children did indeed suffer; they suffered even more if they turned to someone they thought that they could trust for help and were not only not believed, but also rejected – and passed back to the perpetrator to be punished for such ungrateful and wicked lies.

I was at a meeting in East Anglia when a clergyman picked up on remarks that I had made in this vein, and told me of an old lady, totally unknown to him, who had sent for him one day when she felt close to death. She wanted to confess what she had held secret all her life. For seventy years or so she had lived out a lonely, bitter, anti-social existence – you could not call it life. She had not been able to have relationships, she was hostile to all around her – in short she was unloving and unloved. And the reason? As a little girl she had been subjected to sexual abuse by her grandfather, with whom she lived: he would 'play hospitals' with her in the greenhouse. When grandmother found out, far from comforting the child or protecting her, she gave her a thorough whipping, for leading grandfather astray – when she was only six years old. There had been no one she could turn to who would believe her and her whole life was destroyed.

As growing numbers of cases of sexual abuse come to light, many other adults are coming forward to talk, for the first time, of the shame and degradation which they had gone through as children, and of the difficulties with which they had contended as they grew up, tried to form relationships and live natural and fulfilling lives.

A young London woman told me that she had been repeatedly molested by her father when she was small. She had managed to marry and have children, but when she tried to care for them she couldn't; they were taken into the legal custody of their father and she had separated from them. She had now remarried, and as sexual abuse became more recognised, she was developing the strength to tackle her problems and begin to re-start as a wife, and as a mother. Likewise, late in 1987 I was at a public meeting in an industrial town and heard one speaker, a very prominent and respected man in his community, plead for more resources for child abuse work, saying that he himself had been placed in foster care as a boy because he had been so badly neglected. Later he told me privately that he had then run away from foster care, because of sexual abuse. The telephone service ChildLine hears such stories every day, because now that the subject can be talked about these people can at last unburden themselves.

Unfortunately one of the greatest worries about the Cleveland furore in 1987 was that the public reaction to what appeared to be excessive diagnosis and family disruption during an apparent epidemic of sexual abuse, would bring back an atmosphere of rejection, by professionals and public. This fear was borne out for me by the evidence of a colleague, who received a series of telephone calls during the autumn of 1987 from a teenage girl, who told of well-established sexual abuse by her father. She felt that she could cope with this, but was worried for her younger sister, who was beginning to be a victim too. She refused to give any name or address, saying, 'Even if you did get us taken into care, after this Cleveland business we'd only be sent back to him, wouldn't we?' She disappeared, a sad victim of loss of trust in society.

Nevertheless there appears to be public acceptance that sexual abuse does exist. We can be very sure that the sorts of cases of sexual abuse that are now coming to light have been happening to generations of children in the past, when the climate of opinion was such that their plight was an unacceptable concept – therefore it just 'didn't happen'. But even though children are now being believed, and are coming forward in increasing numbers – and many adults also are coming forward to reveal the hidden torments of their own childhoods – we have no sure way of knowing, now that we are at last coming to grips with the problem, whether we are doing so at a time when the actual incidence of cases, as distinct from the numbers coming to light, is much the same, or worse, or better than before. It would be comforting to think that we are at last able to reach out to children and to help them, however imperfectly. But after the greater sexual licence of recent years, and the insidious increase of violence in our society, I do not believe that we can afford to be complacent. The spectre of AIDS adds a new dimension of horror.

With other types of abuse, one of the important points to keep in mind is that we are trying to make comparisons between periods when there were different criteria for defining abuse, different ways of recording it and different standards of what was 'normal'. For instance, in my own lifetime the attitude towards physical punishment has changed dramatically. 'Spare the rod and spoil the child' was very much the theme when I was young, and vigorous physical chastisement was not only acceptable but almost a necessary provision for proper development; nowadays it is practically eliminated in schools, and while still prevalent at home probably less so than ever before.

Poverty continues to be with us – but it is of a different order from the days of appalling slums, widespread malnutrition and ragged children running barefoot in the freezing cold. Some modern dwellings can be slums, full of filth and excrement, with ragged peaky children – but often it is because of idiosyncracy of behaviour by individuals who cannot cope, rather than the norm. The view of what constitutes poverty varies from one generation to another, and so indeed may the definition of cruelty. The plight of children in the infested slums of old was regarded by too many as their 'natural lot'. Attitudes towards their having any rights were at a very elementary stage; today, while there is still a long way to go, there has been significant advance in our way of thinking.

There is the threat of a reaction against children's rights, because of a perceived conflict with the rights of parents. I find this a concept that it is difficult to accept. Children have rights to protection, nourishment, encouragement to develop and loving care. Parents as individuals have their own civic rights, and the expectation that as parents they will be left to raise their children as they think best, within the law and current standards. The only normal conflict between various rights and expectations within a family are those which occur naturally and must be resolved by achieving a balance: not everyone can have a bath at the same time, and if Jane is to have new shoes Jimmy may have to wait for his new rain-coat.

However, parents' rights in regard to their children cannot be divorced from their responsibilities; indeed their rights can be respected only if they discharge their duty to their children to a reasonable degree. Failure to protect, nourish, provide due care – let alone causing harm or distress – can justify intrusion into the privacy of a family so as to protect the rights of the children.

When this privacy is invaded and children and their parents are separated without proper cause, then it is wrong to call this an interference with the rights of the parents, because the children are being wrongly dealt with too: their rights are also being disregarded and the whole family is suffering. This obviously should be avoided if at all possible, and the abuse of the authority to intervene is a shameful thing. I must stress the word 'if', because sometimes the most strident complaint comes from parents who are in fact in the wrong and are putting up a very vigorous counter-attack as a ploy.

Child-care workers can be placed in a very difficult dilemma. There might be suspicion that all is not well within the family; neighbours may report that one of the children has not been seen for days, or had bruises, or was always crying. Should one intervene, perhaps cause great distress, when the reason for what is happening may be perfectly natural? Might there be a risk if the suspicion is ignored that a child's life may be endangered – when it could have been saved? The only way to avoid unhappiness is to take the right decision every time – and that is virtually impossible.

One has to put the interests of children who *may* be at risk before one's own possible discomfort and the risk of causing distress unnecessarily. Most reasonable people accept that this is so – but it can be very difficult indeed to feel like being reasonable when someone you don't know calls and says that there is concern about whether you are being cruel to your children and they would like to have a look, please.

Expectations have changed too in that general standards of health and hygiene have improved greatly during this century and at an apparently accelerating pace the whole time. In the forty years since the National Health Service began there has been a revolution in the provision for monitoring children's progress. Health visitors routinely visit homes when a child is born, and encourage mothers to come regularly to clinics where weight and growth can be checked. Doctors and nurses can give advice, school nurses pick up the surveillance as the children grow. There are still disadvantaged families that slip through the net, but there is a caring network that never was before. Indeed, there are those who suggest that the greater incidence of abuse and neglect in disadvantaged families could be an artefact: they are under the attention of so many professional networks that signs of child abuse may be picked up which would not be noticed in 'better' families – because no one is there to notice, not because they do not occur. It is an interesting point, but difficult to prove.

Another important point to note is that comparisons with the past are difficult to make because there is a lack of comparable statistics. The fact that the NSPCC dealt with 200, or 2,000, or 20,000 cases in a particular year over the last century – and the caseload grew from 1884 until the 1960s – shows only what the workload of that Society was; when it had only a handful of Inspectors, or even when their numbers had climbed to two or three hundred, there could be no expectation that the numbers of children coming to their attention had any relationship or any consistent statistical ratio with the total incidence across England, Wales and

(Northern)[1] Ireland. In 1987 the NSPCC responded in one way or another (for not all were proven abuse) to over 23,000 cases that were referred to its 400 or so social work staff. But as there are no national records nobody knows how many cases were referred to some 25,000 local authority social workers; and without that knowledge there is no way of assessing what the information means.

If the staff of the NSPCC experience an upsurge in cases, as they did, for example, after the Heidi Koseda tragedy, it does not necessarily follow that there are more cases happening, or that a high public awareness has caused more cases to be revealed that were happening all the time. More cases being reported to one agency may mean that some fluctuation in public attitudes means that there are fewer being reported to the social services: the overall numbers could in fact be going down. However, if Social Services Departments are simultaneously experiencing a higher caseload, the implications could be far more serious. That is why it is so desperately important that there should be proper national statistics; they are needed to show changes, for better or worse, in the overall incidence of child abuse; to discern, we hope, the effectiveness of preventive measures; and, also, to help establish what is happening within this overall picture. Is all child abuse increasing? Or is sexual abuse the growth area? Until we have ways of answering such questions the campaign against child cruelty could be working to the wrong priorities.

Isolated data can be produced, but often needs to be interpreted with care. We can be in the position of someone looking at one corner of a complex diagram with a magnifying glass, without having any idea of the whole picture; a little knowledge can indeed be a dangerous thing if we act upon it as though it were the whole truth.

At the present time various estimates of the number of child deaths occurring in the home, because of cruelty, are of the order of 150 to 200 a year; yet the NSPCC calculated that between 1890 and 1900 over 16,000 infants died from one

[1] For many years the NSPCC operated throughout Ireland, until the Irish Society for the Prevention of Cruelty to Children was founded in 1954, in Dublin, and continues to work within the Republic.

cause alone – from being 'overlaid' or smothered in their sleep by often drunken parents or others sharing the same beds.

We do not know, unfortunately, on what data the Victorian death rate was calculated. There is enough difficulty looking at current figures. In 1984 when I announced that at least one child a week died at the hands of its own parents there was frank disbelief in some quarters, and the NSPCC received charges of sensationalism in order to gain funds and public sympathy. Yet I knew that this number of 50 deaths a year was an underestimate. The figure came from an analysis of all the newspaper reports that had been collected, where parents (or parent substitutes) had been convicted of killing their children. But there must have been many cases that did not reach criminal conviction for lack of evidence; or that were not reported; or where death was assumed to be natural, of some underfed and uncared-for baby. Post mortem X-rays might have shown repeated injuries that contributed to death, but had not been recognised as being the underlying cause of, say, pneumonia, which was all that appeared on the death certificate. An attempt to assess the death rate was made in 1985, and Fig. 5 summarises what I consider to be a responsible, but necessarily cautious, estimate.

Nowadays the local authority Social Services Departments have a statutory duty to investigate allegations of child abuse,

	per annum
Registrar-General figures:	
Hunger, thirst, exposure, neglect	19
Homicide + injury purposely inflicted	68
Injury undetermined (suspicious)	49
	136
Estimate that approximately 68% caused by parent or caregiver (68% × 136)	92
'Natural causes' with contributory violence	50
Misdiagnoses	12
	154

FIG. 5 ESTIMATE OF DEATHS FOLLOWING CHILD ABUSE OR
NEGLECT – AVERAGE FOR 1974–85

and by and large they act as custodians of the child abuse registers for their areas. Even though the NSPCC has more social work staff in its 'inspectorate' than at any time in its history, it is very much in the minority as compared with social workers in local authority service, who, while few of them may be child abuse specialists, carry the main burden of child abuse work. The NSPCC continues to record details of all the cases it deals with, but these can in no way be a reliable guide to the overall incidence of child cruelty.

For rather over a decade the most reliable index that has been available has been provided by the NSPCC, on a different basis. There are some local authority areas where the NSPCC is the contracting agency which maintains the child abuse register as part of its involvement. Because the criteria used are the same for all the NSPCC registers it is possible to aggregate the figures from each of these registers and create a large sample. Each local authority works within a defined geographical area with a known population, and thus we can establish that the total child population in the areas covered by the NSPCC-maintained registers is 9.6 per cent of the total child population of England and Wales.

This sample is fortuitous rather than statistically 'random', and it may not be truly representative. Nevertheless, estimates of national occurrence based upon its aggregate figures provide a reasonable guide as to the overall picture; perhaps more significantly, changes from year to year in the fifteen years that this research has been in progress give a reliable assessment of trends. Indeed, it is as 'Trends in Child Abuse' that these figures are published, forming the largest ongoing survey that exists.

Nevertheless it is clear that there is an urgent need for more comprehensive statistics. The Society has been pressing for many years for a proper, government-backed, national survey, and in July 1987 the Health Minister announced that the Department of Health and Social Security would be initiating such a development. Now that the government has acknowledged the need, one hopes that action will not be far away.

Meanwhile we have to rely on the NSPCC figures. What do

they tell us? In 1987 there were 2,304 children placed on the child abuse registers within the NSPCC sample, which suggests that for England and Wales as a whole the known ('discovered') rate of established child abuse and neglect affects something like 25,000 children a year. (Figures of this order are confirmed in a recent survey by the Association of Directors of Social Services.) This gives us some idea of the size of problem that we have to face – and find the resources for. But what do these figures mean – and how do they compare with previous years?

The breakdown of cases is given in Fig. 6. The first point that becomes apparent is that about a quarter of the entries were of children who, while at such high risk that it was thought necessary to place their names on the register, had no actual proven injury or other abuse; this leaves the figure of 1,656 who were actually abused – which would be about 18,000 nationally. More than half of these children suffered from deliberate physical injuries, about one third suffered from sexual abuse and about a tenth were diagnosed as cases of neglect or failure to thrive. Emotional abuse is represented by a very small fraction – but then it is a very difficult matter to prove. These figures suggest that over 8,000 children a year are physically abused in their own home environment in

	1987	%
Physically injured		
Fatal	8	(0.3)
Serious	103	(4.5)
Moderate	696	(30.2)
Failure to Thrive	50	(2.2)
Sexual Abuse	639	(27.7)
Neglect	126	(5.5)
Emotional Abuse	34	(1.5)
'At risk' cases	648	(28.1)
TOTAL REGISTERED	2304	(100)

FIG. 6 NUMBER OF REGISTERED CHILDREN BY TYPE AND SEVERITY OF ABUSE – 1987

England and Wales, and over 7,000 are sexually abused. A number of people feel that these are underestimates, and they may be right – all that these figures reveal is the incidence of cases that have come to light, because no one knows how many undiscovered cases there may be, or if they exist.

There is a further difficulty in the interpretation of figures, both because the criteria for registration vary in detail (although this should not matter too much because the NSPCC sample is to uniform standards) and also because the content of different registers varies: sexual abuse was not included when the register system began, and when the government issued new advice in 1980 it was left to individual authorities whether they introduced sexual abuse to their own registers or not. Similarly, emotional abuse is difficult to define, recognise or prove, and we know well that neglect is an underrecognised area of child cruelty.

We have felt easiest when looking at the incidence and varying patterns of physical abuse: we know it best, we think we understand it best – it is after all what most people regard as child cruelty – and we have the most comprehensive data. For some years now we have felt some satisfaction in the way that the register figures have shown an increase in the number of cases coming to light, but a decrease in the category of severe/fatal cases.

This trend was so consistent that it appeared to demonstrate that in areas where there was a well coordinated child abuse system across the professional community, which had the confidence to achieve cooperation and public trust, more cases were being brought to light, and brought to light earlier, and fewer were deteriorating into more extreme violence or reaching fatal outcomes. As earlier research had shown a tendency for physical abuse to begin with minor injuries and proceed in many cases to progressively more severe attacks, this was an encouraging development, we hoped. But then, suddenly, the rate of reporting of severe or fatal cases began to go up. Was this just a passing variation that did not mean any reversal of the trend? Or did it mean that our assumptions were wrong?

We just did not know. In any series of figures over a

number of years there will be the likelihood of the occasional reading being out of line, even if the general trend is in fact unchanged, and it is necessary to keep apparent changes in perspective until their meaning becomes clearer. At the same time, when the well-being of children is at stake, it is important to be alert to possible changes in trends; certainly it is always advisable to try to avoid sitting back and feeling complacent.

In this case there are three main possibilities as to why the number of cases reported went up. The trend towards better and earlier discovery, and achieving therefore better protection from serious outcomes, is the one that we hope for. There is the possibility that in a society which is becoming more inured to violence there is in fact a greater actual incidence of physical abuse of children. The third option is a personal observation, made by doctors and social workers with day-to-day experience, that the pattern of injury is changing: that is to say, the 'crescendo effect' of minor irritation with baby leading to minor violence, and baby's failure to respond leading to increasingly savage blows, may be less apparent; some workers feel that they are seeing more cases where severe and potentially fatal major injury is the first sign of abuse. We cannot be sure of the validity of any of these observations; we can only be vigilant and try to improve how we interpret information, as well as improve the quality of information that comes in.

The data is all the more difficult to interpret because of the many different trends going on in our society – and, therefore, the many temptations to 'blame' one upon another, when their different interactions may be far less definite. For instance, for years the NSPCC has found that 'marital discord' has been the most consistent 'stress factor' in families where there are cases of child abuse. This could be interpreted as showing that stress between man and wife results in their taking it out on the children; but it could also mean that people who have difficulty in their relationships with their partners also have difficulty in their management of their children. It is impossible to say whether one results from the other or whether they both have a common cause.

High rise flats were identified in NSPCC research as providing an environment that seemed to encourage child abuse. It was easy to see why. Families that were moved from crowded slums, where conditions were bad but there was plenty of human contact, felt themselves isolated in flats that were modern but high up and cut off. Children could not be let out of the front door, lest they fall to their deaths. Until they were old enough there was no hope of letting them go down to ground level unsupervised and let off steam in a playground. If the lift broke down or was vandalised there was little chance of getting a pram, baby, laundry and shopping up the stairs – down was bad enough. In consequence mothers became prisoners, trapped in their flats, with no one to lean out and chat to – and with the children under their feet all day long, lacking fresh air and exercise. No wonder nerves became frayed, children fretful and full of minor complaints, relations between parents suffered – and it was taken out on the children. But this happened in only some, not all, families.

Unemployment has grown significantly in the past decade, even if there is now a prospect that it may be falling. Unemployment has also shown the greatest rate of increase of all the stress factors associated with child abuse. There are those who maintain that the stresses of being made unemployed can result in more abuse of children, while others argue that when troubles hit a family the first thought in most cases is that the children must not suffer.

There is another factor here. 'The unemployed' are not a simple homogeneous sector of society, but include those fresh from school seeking jobs, some who are unexpectedly redundant who will soon find another post – and others who won't; those who have been waiting in dread for their jobs to go so that life is almost more bearable (at first, anyway) when the worst does happen; those who have lost hope of getting back into regular employment; those who always have been virtually unemployable. Quite apart from their individual attitudes and backgrounds, which will affect how they respond in any case, the nature of their unemployment is likely to have an influence on how they react. Dr Taitz and his colleagues in Sheffield published an article in the *British Medical Journal* in April 1987 in which they concluded, from their experience in that city, that there was no evidence that the recent increase in unemployment had had any appreciable effect upon the incidence of child abuse.

Again, there is probably a variety of patterns within an apparent trend. While in many families unemployment can mean better parenting because both parents can share more fully in caring for their children, there may be others where the depressant effect of feeling worthless can have the effect of certain parents becoming irritated by their children and abusing them – but there is often some other factor as well. At the other extreme those who have chronic difficulty in holding down a job may also have difficulty in coping with the 'job' of rearing children. I do not see how one can pontificate, however great the emotional satisfaction, and produce telling statements which over-simplify a complex of issues. Likewise with considerations of race; nowadays information on ethnic background is collected, but as there are local variations in populations and local comparative information is not readily available, we are unable to say whether any particular groups are over or under represented.

To take this subject further requires a more specialist approach than is appropriate for this book; but I hope that I have been able to give some general impression of the trends in child abuse statistics as they appear at present, and a broad understanding of the difficulty in interpreting them. When the government at last proceed with developing records as a national register we will be in a better position in future years to begin to develop a clearer understanding; meanwhile, whilst there are many unknown factors, we can be sure of a commonly observed phenomenon: whenever child abuse is in the news, the number of cases being reported goes up. Year by year, if you chart the daily number of new cases and check what was in the news at times when there are peaks on the chart, you will find that there has been a tragic death, a well-publicised court case or a major press statement which has brought the subject home to millions of listeners or readers. This was demonstrated to me by one of my staff whom I happened to meet the day after I had been broadcasting about child abuse matters. He told me he had heard me on his car radio when driving to a case. 'Crikey!' he had thought to himself, 'The guv'nor on the radio — that will mean more cases in the next few days!'

It always seems sad that it can take a horrific child death to stimulate people who know of a child abuse problem to decide to do something about it, although reticence about 'interfering' is very understandable. But what I find encouraging about the greater public attention being given to abuse these days is that we are able to say with some confidence that, whether the incidence of child abuse in its various forms is going up, down or staying fairly static, the reporting rate is going up: and that this is in part at least the result of having a better informed and more understanding general public.

Chapter Four: **Neglect**

For many years, neglect has formed the largest single area of work recorded by the NSPCC. Fig. 1 on page 13 shows how new referrals in 1987 outnumbered all other types of case, and in Fig. 7 this comparison is extended over the previous eight years.

If there is so much of it about, why is neglect so little heard of? While recent publicity, such as the NSPCC 'Forgotten Children' campaign of 1986, has helped to raise the level of

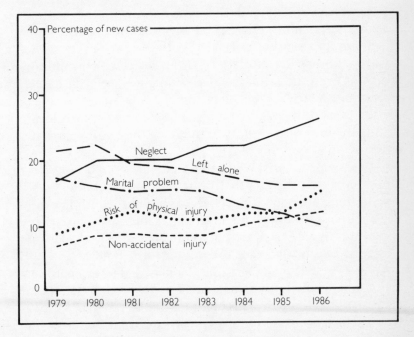

FIG. 7   CLASSIFICATION OF NEW CASES 1979–1986

public awareness of this form of child cruelty, it seldom comes across with the drama of some of the highlighted physical cruelty cases which stir up such strong public reaction.

I think that there are several reasons why this should be so. Perhaps one is that child abuse is generally seen as somebody doing something – either being wilfully cruel to a child, or performing a deliberate act such as an angry shaking which is not meant to harm as severely as, tragically, may happen. Neglect is failing to do or provide something necessary for a child's well-being, and whether this is because of ignorance or thoughtlessness the impact on public consciousness is more low key; would that this were so for the helpless child. Where, as in the case of Malcolm Page in Essex who died of cold, hunger and neglect (whose circumstances I shall consider later) or Heidi Koseda in Hillingdon, whose ill treatment and neglect resulted in her death and whose dead body lay undetected for many weeks in the family's home, there is deliberate privation resulting in drawn-out death, there certainly will be a public outcry.

Neglect can kill – and this is not only in the cases of deliberate starvation. There is no way of knowing how many times an apparently 'normal' death, say from bronchopneumonia, has had neglect as an unsuspected contributory factor, or even the primary cause. It might have been neglect in feeding, which lowers resistance in a wasted little body; neglect in clothing or providing adequate warmth; neglect in getting medical care in time, or in giving the treatment that is ordered.

While neglect can be life-threatening in such ways, we must not ignore the fact that even if we do not know its full extent, there are many thousands of children who suffer from neglect in lesser forms which can blight their lives in so many different ways. Moreover, different forms of cruelty do not exist in isolation from each other. One form of abuse can lead to another: the late Dr Christine Cooper used to estimate that about one case in five that came to her paediatric clinic because of neglect had signs of injury due to physical abuse as well. (They would not always be apparent without full examination and bone X-rays.)

One problem in establishing whether neglect exists is that many children may fail to thrive in their physical development because of 'natural causes' such as unsuspected underlying disease, and need careful medical assessment, in which case there need be no neglect.

A little while ago one of our Inspectors in Hampshire had a telephone call from a petty criminal whose family he knew well. Mr Hardy had been arrested and expected a prison sentence. 'Keep an eye on the kids for me,' was what he wanted to say.

So the Inspector went to have a look at the family. The general standard of care for the children was anything but good, and their dispirited mother was on the downward spiral of lack of confidence leading to incompetent performance which in turn lowered her self-esteem – and so reduced her self-confidence even more. However, there was nothing actually wrong with the family – except that the baby looked very peaky and underweight. A doctor was called in.

Medical examination soon established that this was no case of neglect: baby was ill with coeliac disease, a condition when the digestive system cannot cope with ordinary foods and a special diet is needed. But here was a mother without the first idea of how to feed normal children properly, let alone provide a special diet.

The centre where this Inspector worked was in a house which had been made available by the local authority, and where local supporters had helped to furnish and equip it – even provide a fully fitted kitchen where young mothers could be taught simple home management. This proved to be very useful. With the help of a dietician from the local Gas Board this young mother was given special tuition in how to obtain and prepare her baby's special food. It meant a lot to her that for once somebody thought that she mattered enough to give her this attention, and she responded with growing interest. No miracle happened overnight, but she became able to look after her baby effectively, which in turn gave such a boost to her morale that her 'downward spiral' was stopped. She began to take an interest in looking after her other children – and in herself and her appearance. It was a slow climb up, but the confidence which came from getting something right, and from being supported and encouraged, helped her to begin to develop some self-respect and to go on improving her performance. She had been as much neglected as she was neglectful, but with the right intervention she could begin to respond.

There can of course be an almost endless range of 'mixed causes', whereby a medical condition may indeed be responsible for a child's failure to thrive, but that such a condition occurred, or was not dealt with sooner, or did not have persistence in treatment, may be partly or wholly due to neglect on the part of the parents.

Such neglected children are all the more prone to any infection – and have very little resistance. Minor illness that the average child could throw off without a thought can be life-threatening to a child who has not the bodily strength or nourishment for its own protective mechanisms to work; that has neither the cleanliness nor warmth to help its little body to survive; that lacks the love that can give it any will to live.

A helpful report published in 1988 by the Children's Research Fund, entitled 'The Medical Aspects of Child Abuse', gives a very helpful resumé of the related problems of neglect, failure to thrive and impaired development. It makes the telling remark that 'the opposite of love is not hate but indifference'; babies need to be stimulated as well as provided for if they are to develop, and being left alone with a bottle balanced on a pillow is not an inducement to develop normally, nor to take an interest in life. Surveillance of young children to show whether they are reaching the expected milestones in weight, height, movement and speech is very important, and one of the challenges to health visitors who have such a key role to play is in finding the children who are slipping through the net of being seen for their routine checks. Some children fail to thrive because they have one of a variety of diseases; others are in effect apathetic about growing because they are treated with apathy.

The differential diagnosis of the various causes of failure to thrive is a matter for medical and nursing textbooks rather than this book but a few words about the charting of infant development may be helpful. Children – like their parents – vary enormously in height and weight and in their rate of development. A child may seem scrawny and underweight for its age, but granny will say, 'He's just like his father, and his grandfather too, from all I've heard,' and granny may yet again be right. But there are norms, and all children should show a rate of development in weight and height that, whatever the individual variation, is within a broad range of recorded values. These are charted, showing the average rate, and the variations by percentage figures that are within the bounds of acceptability; they are called 'Percentile Charts'.

Fig. 8 shows a typical percentile chart. All children, unless they are ill or being deprived of adequate nourishment for growth, should fall within the 30 per cent variations above and below the average of 50 per cent. Most fall within 10 per cent above or below. If a child falls ill and has to go into

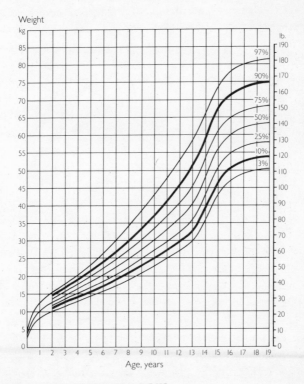

FIG. 8 PERCENTILE CHART FOR BOYS

hospital, the normal expectation would be for the child temporarily to go off his or her food, showing a drop in weight (or a failure to go on gaining weight) compared with the chart. Where there is neglect which involves gross malnutrition, this expectation is reversed, and the child actually gains weight whilst in hospital (or other) care – only to lose again on being allowed home, suggesting that there is something wrong with the child's care, not the child. This is one of the most telling tests of neglect. I am grateful to Dr Peter Barbor for Fig. 9 which makes this very point. The inquiry into the death of Jasmine Beckford ('A Child in Trust', 1985) dealt with the matter at some length, stressing the unique value of this method of recording and interpreting information.

The case of Alan and Andrew who lived in an industrial city in the Midlands illustrates some of these points. Alan was a little boy of two who was thought to be failing to thrive and the NSPCC was asked to visit. The Inspector found a

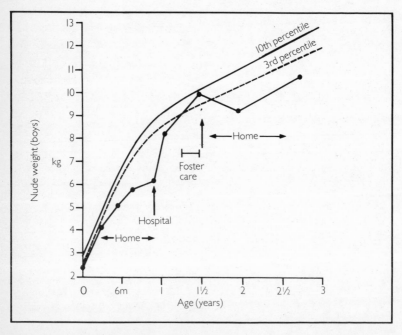

FIG. 9   PERCENTILE CHART SHOWING FLUCTUATIONS IN WEIGHT AND INADEQUATE GROWTH AT HOME

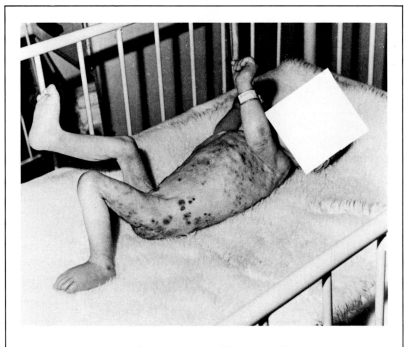

1. Chronic neglect still exists — this emaciated child is also suffering from neglected nappy rash

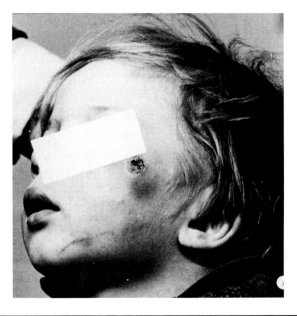

2. The distinctive form of a cigarette burn: note the sharp definition. Bruises are also present

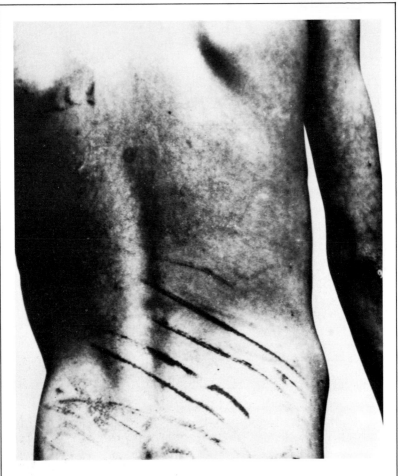

3. *The marks of abuse: this child has been whipped*

4. This child was sat on an electric ring; note burns too to his fingers. This type of injury is sometimes inflicted as a punishment for soiling

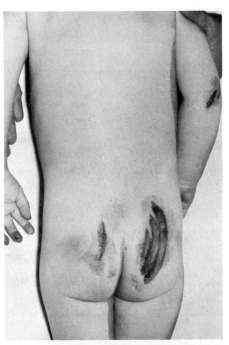

5. Bruising, the result of substantial blows to the head

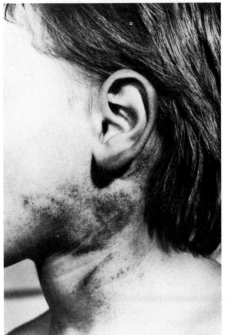

6. *Soiled and saturated bedding. How can any child feel loved and cared for when left in such circumstances?*

7. *Filth and squalor which gradually build to quite unacceptable levels due to apathy, ignorance and indifference of parents. This kitchen is unhygienic and dangerous; it was nonetheless being used by a family*

reasonably clean home, but parents who seemed to have no real interest in their child; they left him in a cot in an otherwise empty room and they never took him out.

Alan seemed very small for his age, and the Inspector was concerned that he seemed so unresponsive. Jangling a bunch of keys usually excites a baby's interest, but Alan did not respond at all, and the Inspector suggested that he should go with the parents to the hospital for Alan to have a thorough medical and developmental examination. The parents refused; they said that Alan was perfectly healthy and did not need any medical attention. The mother was pregnant and her husband complained that 'all this fuss' was causing her unnecessary strain.

The Inspector discussed the case with his Team Leader and successfully applied for a Place of Safety Order from a local magistrate. Alan spent a week in hospital, where tests showed his height and weight to be those of a child of about thirteen months – half his age. Intellectually and emotionally he was even more retarded.

The child then went to stay with very experienced foster parents. A rapid transformation began to take place: he put on weight; he began to grow; instead of spending most of his time lying inert in his cot he began to take a very real interest in people and objects around him. He was beginning to catch up with normal development.

The Society tried to obtain a Care Order for Alan. His parents contested this, and a series of Interim Orders was obtained. Meanwhile a second child was born, another boy – Andrew. Neither parent showed any sign of having learned any more about child care and there was considerable anxiety about their ability to cope with the new baby.

At the final hearing of the Care Proceedings on Alan's case, the NSPCC called the hospital paediatrician, the family doctor, a health visitor and a social worker from the local authority fostering and adoption team to give evidence before the magistrates, and the social worker who had been appointed *guardian ad litem* for Alan provided a report. The magistrates were so concerned that they made Care Orders in respect of both children.

Alan and Andrew are both now with foster parents. Alan continues to make excellent progress and Andrew is developing normally. Both are enjoying their world.

It is no light decision to remove a new baby from its natural mother, but in the light of the experience of Alan's case, and of the failure of the parents to make any move to change, it was undoubtedly right that Andrew should be spared the neglectful and damaging upbringing that Alan had experienced and have a chance to make a proper start in life in a stable and loving home. Also, it has been shown that neglect, like most forms of abuse except sexual, affects more boys than girls, and that it more usually occurs in the youngest child of a larger family than with the first-born.

That the NSPCC in the early days of its existence in Victorian England should have seen countless cases of young children brought up in the squalor and filth of Dickensian depiction is understandable — indeed, its work might be caricatured as only such. To find such conditions in the Britain of today would seem remarkable — who could believe that plates 6, 7 and 8 could have been taken in recent times? Yet they were. Sadly, even today it is all too possible to find such cases.

Malcolm Page died in Essex in bitterly cold weather during the winter of 1979. The conditions shown at post-mortem included severe malnutrition, gangrene and hypothermia. The report of a panel of inquiry published by Essex County Council included a description of the rooms in the house where he had lived, which says in part:

3.94 In the remaining bedroom there was a single bed with a single mattress. The mattress was sodden in urine, there was a coloured blanket on the bed and that was also sodden with urine. There was a torn sheet similarly wet. The carpet contained evidence of excrement having been trodden in it and there were also lumps of excrement on the floor. There was a biscuit tin which had paper on top. When the paper was removed there was evidence of excrement in the biscuit tin. There were fifteen empty milk bottles on the floor of the room in different positions.

3.95 The smell on the upstairs floor changed from one of a very strong urine smell to foul smell from the rotting excrement.

There were similar descriptions of the other rooms; four people had lived there.

In a recent television interview one of our Team Leaders told of visiting a home where a very neglected baby was lying in a foul urine-soaked cot. Mother seemed unconcerned, so the Team Leader asked her to put her face down on the cot pillow where the baby lay. The ammoniacal smell from decomposing urine was so strong that the mother's eyes watered, and only then did she begin to understand that she was doing something wrong.

Very often such physical neglect stems from sad ignorance of what a baby needs. Foster parents of an abused child were horrified whenever they handed the baby over to its natural mother for the permitted outings to find that the clean child with a bottle of milk that they parted with was such an unhappy little wretch when she was returned, angrily sucking at a bottle of cold tea, with her nappy unchanged all day.

So often the difficulty is a self-perpetuating one. The unskilled young mother who cannot cope might well have had too many children too quickly, and any hope of her coming to learn how to manage with a single child can be swamped by the burden of coping with so many. A further calamity, like her husband losing his job, or mounting debts, or the cooker packing up, can precipitate a crisis quite beyond her capacity to manage. She feels hopeless and helpless, and the rejection by her neighbours of her noisome brood just accelerates the downward spiral of diminishing self-confidence or self-esteem, leading to even poorer performance – and so on.

In cases of neglected children sometimes the cause is ignorance, the inability to care properly, apathy or a hopelessness about being able to care; alternatively it might be a wilful indifference as to whether the children receive any care or not. For instance, the mother who fed tea to her baby had never been able to bring up a child on her own, and just had no idea of what to feed. Equally ignorant was the mother of two little boys in a playgroup who were asked what they had for breakfast. 'Oxo, as usual,' they replied. How did mum give it to them? In a bowl with bread? 'No, from the wrapper.' One dry beef cube was what mum had thought to be a square meal. On the other hand, the little girl pictured in plate 12 was subjected to a callous indifference that was not just through ignorance. The starved neglected skeleton of a child was deliberately and wilfully deprived of food and gained what nourishment it could to keep alive by scavenging in dustbins. However, it is not always easy to draw such a clear line between these two types of neglect.

There are many other stories of harmful lack of care. The NSPCC received a report in London that two girls, about two and three years old, were rarely seen during the day and looked undernourished. A social worker called, and received no reply; all the curtains were drawn. She called again later and still had no response, but she glimpsed a child's face at a window. She called again later on and was let in by the mother, who was very cross that someone had told the NSPCC.

She denied that she spent all day in bed, and said that her younger child Jane would soon be going to day nursery, and the older, Paula was due to start school. Jane was indeed five years old, but was so small and undernourished that she looked more like a three-year-old. She had something in her hand which the Inspector realised was a raw beefburger: her mother was angry and said she must have stolen it from the kitchen but when she tried to take it away Jane refused to let go. Clearly she was very hungry.

The Inspector discovered that the children were sleeping all day and awake all night to fit in with their mother's lifestyle. When Jane and Paula were later medically examined they were found to be significantly underweight for their age.

Extensive attempts to help the mother improve her care of the children were unsuccessful, so the Society decided to take legal action in order to make sure that they were looked after properly. Both girls were made the subjects of Care Orders by the court, and placed with foster parents, where the work of rehabilitating them could begin.

It might well be asked why so much time is spent trying to redeem such hopeless situations. 'The parents are obviously inadequate and should never be allowed to have charge of children', it may be said; 'The sooner those little mites are taken into care the better.'

Judged with hindsight, that may indeed be so. At the time, however, it is not easy, nor may it be right in the interests of the children to take precipitate action. There is some sort of relationship, there may be elements of love and of caring – and it may be the only relationship, the only security, that the children know. Is it better to try to build on that, and try to make the home and the parents the children know and belong to into a better and more caring environment, or to break them off from all their roots and hope that something better will be achieved? There may be no right course, just a difficult decision as to which is the least wrong one.

So often the parents, too, are the victims of circumstances not of their making. Their own upbringing may have been equally bizarre and inadequate, and any attempts they may have made to do a bit better may have been thwarted by misfortune or ignorance; being inured to a state of hopelessness may leave them passive, resigned and apathetic. The children must come first, in all our work, but the parents have rights and expectations too, and the ideal to aim at is to try to bring these together. Consider the following case, which was brought to the attention of the NSPCC in East Anglia by an anonymous telephone call from a neighbour. She was worried that the children were living in terrible conditions, they had no proper sleeping accommodation, they smelt and their general care was poor.

The Society's Officer found that a single parent family with five children, with ages ranging from twelve to one, was living in a ground floor flat. The garden was unkempt and piled high with rubbish, and the inside of the flat was almost unbelievable. Every room was filthy, with piles of rotting refuse and dirty clothing everywhere.

In the bedrooms it was difficult to see where the children actually slept and some of the beds were wet. The kitchen and bathroom were particularly bad: the kitchen floor was covered with uneaten food, empty milk bottles and cartons were strewn all over the place, and as tins had been opened the empties were discarded around the floor. The cooker did not work and the refrigerator was green with mould and slime. While the bathroom appeared to be in use it was dirty and unhygienic and the toilet was almost overflowing. A sickly nauseating smell pervaded everywhere and clung to the Inspector's clothes when he got home.

In the middle of all this were five children – mucky, smelly, but apparently happy. The youngest seemed the most vulnerable, moving from one sister or brother to another for attention.

According to the mother, Mrs Wilson, things had begun to go from bad to worse following the birth of the baby, Thomas. Her husband had already left her, the birth had been a difficult one and she had had post-natal depression. For a while she had tried to get things a bit better, but in the last six months or so she had just let go and everything had built up around her; although she had never been much of a housekeeper, things had never been as bad as this. What came across was that the mother had put all her energies into the children. They all seemed fairly happy, and had a sense of family togetherness; they also seemed remarkably healthy under the circumstances.

The Inspector went into action and promptly contacted all the professional agencies that needed to be involved. The Environmental Health Officer declared the house unfit for habitation, and temporary accommodation was sought so that the mother and her five children could be kept together if possible. At a case conference it was agreed that the relationships within the family were such that they should indeed be kept together, their home should be cleaned out and refurbished, and that they should be supported in trying to make a better go of things.

A plan of action over the next four weeks led to the house being fumigated, cleared out, redecorated and refurnished. While this was going on, better assessments could be made of the family, their relationships, their strengths and their failings. There was an obvious close bond between Mrs

Wilson and her children, and between all the children. They all began to respond to being offered such positive help and became very excited about the work being done on their home.

Thanks to excellent cooperation between all the agencies taking part, and a well-managed coordination of all the different services, the plan was completed to schedule, and all the furniture, bedding, clothing and other necessities were there on time.

An excited and happy family moved back to their newly smart home. There were immediate signs that they were taking responsibility for keeping it up to a reasonable standard, and while it was necessary to monitor the situation for some time (in a way that would help them without making them become permanently dependent) Mrs Wilson willingly responded to support and guidance, and her older children were helped to share some of the responsibility with her.

But for all these hopeful cases there are many more that reflect a lesser degree of lack of care; where there is food, but of a quality and monotony that deny normal healthy growth; where there is care of a sort, but the whole experience of upbringing leads to an apathetic inadequacy to do other than succumb to precocious pregnancy which leads to inability to care for the new baby – and another generation in turn suffers its blighted lives. What can be done about it?

Investigating Physical Neglect

I am grateful to Mr Robin Wratten for the checklist of observations to be made on a home visit when neglect is alleged, which appears in Appendix III. This was produced during the time that he ran the Family Centre at the NSPCC Unit in Northamptonshire, and gives an idea of the comprehensive approach that needs to be made in investigating child abuse cases. For those who do not need to study it in detail it will help if we look at some selected highlights.

Clothing may be both inadequate and inappropriate, as we have seen in some of the case examples, and might be too cool in winter, or too hot in summer. Protecting from the heat is less often considered than wrapping up in cold weather, but it was not very long ago that the NSPCC prosecuted a doctor and his wife for leaving their baby in an unventilated car on a blazing hot day – it might have died but for the actions of a passer-by.

Hygiene: adults, children or clothing may be dirty and smelly; there may be no soap, flannels, toothbrushes or other basic essentials. This is not just a matter of poverty in material terms – more often a matter of poverty of spirit: a lack of pride, of self-esteem. The key to achieving change is that there needs to be a pay-off for the parents, such as enhancing their self-respect. We saw in the case of the baby with coeliac disease (p. 51) how the achievement in coping with a special diet gave the mother a sufficient boost for her to have the incentive to build up her self-esteem with other achievements.

The state of the home may not only show soiled and broken furniture, damaged doors and windows, etc., but also damaged stairs, broken glass on the floor, poisonous solvents and cleaning fluids, unprotected fires, discarded cigarettes, matches, and other hazards, all of which are a great danger to children. It is worrying not just that such obvious dangers should exist when there are children who need to be protected from them; what is also disquieting, and can be soul-destroying to any concerned worker trying to achieve change, is the lack of any apparent concern or interest in taking precautions on the part of neglectful parents.

This disregard can be seen in a variety of ways. There can be an indifference to providing meals – an attitude of 'If a child is hungry, let it fend for itself.' It is not unknown to find some little tots cooking for themselves on the element of an upturned electric fire. There can be no regard for a child's achievements at home, or at school – indeed there may be no interest in taking a child to school or meeting him or her when school is over; teachers come to recognise the children no one ever calls for. Such indifference can be seen in a child's lack of development; no one bothers to unstrap her from her pushchair, or baby is just left lying in a soaking cot, with no stimulus to take an interest, as we saw in the case of Andrew and Alan (page 54).

While it can be too easy to make snap judgments, it seems that there is so often an apparent resistance to any change; a comfortable attitude that what you don't notice – don't want to notice – isn't there, and you don't have to do anything about it; an apathy and indifference. 'Why don't you wipe that child's nose?' 'What for? If I do it'll only run again!' It can be hard to try to persevere in the face of such inertia.

This weary apathy can make any attempt to achieve change seem futile, and well-intentioned social workers can feel overwhelmed with the apparent hopelessness of getting anywhere. An immature young mother, burdened with a feckless or criminal husband, who began her married life with all too little in social or domestic skills, has too many children – and too quickly – and becomes submerged. In such a case there can be an imperceptible deterioration, as inevitable as ageing – and equally unlikely to be noticed by someone in daily contact.

What has been poor but acceptable may deteriorate because some disaster strikes, like serious injury to the husband, or a depressive illness following childbirth; or the scene may worsen so slowly that it is well-nigh impossible to decide when mediocrity of care becomes neglect or to be confident when to intervene into the privacy of a family because the needs – the rights – of the children are being unjustifiably subordinate to the rights of the parents.

The fact always needs to be remembered that neglect *is* a form of abuse, and that neglectful families may commit other forms of abuse as well. Checking the health of an under-nourished and neglected baby includes checking for other problems: the chest X-ray may show not only a lung infection, but a series of rib fractures at different stages of healing because they were inflicted on different occasions. The radiologist – the X-ray specialist – has an important role in detecting child abuse, as Dr Griffiths and Dr Moynihan wrote with great emphasis and understanding in an article in the *British Medical Journal* twenty-five years ago (p. 82).

The degree of health care of the children in a family is

important in itself, and a helpful guide to the attitude of their parents. Many families can go through phases where there seems to be one illness after another; there need be nothing whatever inadequate about parental care, and after a while the children are rarely seen in surgery again. Others, however, have on-going lingering sickness, that may have too little attention too late and which, allied with other findings and the perceived attitude of the parents, point to neglect on their part. Have the children been brought for their regular check-ups, for their immunisations, for the health visitor or clinic nurse to check their progress in growth, weight and other landmarks?

Suspicion of neglect, and its insidious development, needs 'hard' facts to be confirmed. The recording of weight and height can show on the percentile charts I have mentioned; and there are other measurements of progress and attainments that can be used, and measured against the norm, like the Family Health Scales devised by Dr Bentovim and his colleagues at Great Ormond Street Hospital for Sick Children. The health visitor, the family doctor and the social worker all have key roles in watching out for children who do not seem to be getting the care that they should, who are not being brought for their routine attendances, who do not seem to be responding to treatment when it has been prescribed for them – perhaps because no one has been giving it, or persisting for long enough.

The following case was brought to the attention of the NSPCC by the vigilance of someone responsible for children's welfare. A school in the East Midlands noticed how pale a girl of six was. When the headmistress questioned the girl she said, 'Mummy put me under the stairs when I didn't get the washing in.'

When an Inspector visited the mother, Mrs Carter, she broke down and cried and said that her husband had deserted her and gone off with her best friend, she had a small baby as well as the girl and the only way that she could cope when they both started playing up was to lock the little girl in the bedroom. However, the last time she did that the girl tried to get out of the window so she felt the safest place was to put her in the cupboard under the stairs. She said that she had only done this once.

Mrs Carter had been brought to snapping point when she went out shopping and told the child to get the washing in if it started to rain. When the mother returned it was raining and the girl had not got the washing in and that brought her, she said, to screaming pitch: if she had not put the child into the cupboard she would have beaten her. She admitted that the child had been locked in the cupboard for most of the weekend from the Friday to the Sunday evening.

Mrs Carter was counselled in the strictest terms but was also helped with her financial difficulties. Together with the health visitor and a befriender (a middle-aged mother figure) a supportive network was set up to which mother responded in a very positive way. Eventually, the NSPCC was able to close the case with the befriender and the health visitor still monitoring. The children became happier, the mother became more settled and able to cope with her situation and said that she would like to meet the person who reported her to the NSPCC to thank them because we had done so much for her.

Another problem area is that of leaving alone. How old should a child or children be before they can be left alone – for a few minutes while mother nips next door for the loan of an ironing board, or for a longer period to have her hair done? How old should a child be to be left in charge of other children? There cannot be any simple answers. The maturity of children varies enormously and judgments have to be made about how far one should be stimulating greater independence and feelings of responsibility, and how much one is putting children at risk. It is legal for children under sixteen to be left in charge of younger children – one can undoubtedly get away with younger baby-sitters – until something goes wrong, when parents will be held responsible.

The dangers of leaving children alone were tragically brought home to us all following the abduction of three-year-old Leoni Keating. She had been staying in a caravan with her mother whilst on holiday at Great Yarmouth.

On the last night of the family's holiday Mrs Keating had

gone out to a discotheque leaving Leoni in her pyjamas waiting for a baby-sitter. The baby-sitter never arrived and when mother eventually returned to the caravan at 1 a.m. she found that Leoni was missing.

A massive search was mounted and Leoni was found four days later in a water-filled ditch over seventy miles from where she had disappeared. She was dead, her hands tied behind her back. She had drowned and she had also been cruelly sexually abused.

What an appalling death, which would not have occurred if very basic safeguards had been taken; she should never have been left on her own as there was always a risk she might have wandered off, and parents should realise the additional risk that molesters prey on vulnerable young children.

Any responsible parent needs to be aware of what hazards there are about the home and either remove them or make them safe from children; this can be done by putting them out of reach, or by devices such as a gate across the stairs. There needs always to be an awareness that children may be vulnerable and parents must be self-questioning: are there dangerous medicines within reach? Is the house secure and are the children trained in *not* opening the door? There must be literally millions of occasions every year when children are safely and responsibly left on their own, but there are many others when needless risks are taken; parents may get smug because they get away with it, but what is at risk is the life of a child. How often do we see news reports such as 'Three children die in house blaze; parents were out'?

Ways of Effecting Change

Different ways in which change can be effected in neglectful families have already been demonstrated in some of the case examples I have quoted.

Providing material help can be a successful start. So often the suspicion and distrust which, understandably, a family may show to any intruder, however well-intentioned, can be overcome by an approach which is authoritative, rather than authoritarian (which is another way of saying that the professional worker avoids being bossy, but uses the natural authority of knowing his or her job and having a definite goal in focusing upon the child) and which is accompanied by a clear commitment to provide practical help.

The family that was in a terrible mess, but which still was functioning as a family, responded to being given a break from their sordid surroundings and seeing these transformed into a clean and comfortable home (page 59); they still needed somebody around to guide them, but they responded by working to improve their own standards.

The respite that can come from the child or children going to hospital for assessment and immediate attention to any current illness, or from providing temporary foster care whilst problems are being explored and tackled, can provide a welcome relief for parents who have become overwhelmed and so past caring or coping. When the parents can see the action as part of a purposeful plan to which they have contributed, and when they are made to feel that they matter, they can begin to have the incentive to try to improve their competence.

Another valuable asset is the day nursery, or special playgroup/family centre. A child or children going out of the home for regular periods of day care can mean a break for a mother who needs room for herself and time to cope with other demands upon her. It means a break for each child, and a chance to develop in a play-school atmosphere with other children. This is not only valuable for the child, but as we have seen with Kate and Mandy (page 5), it can give mother a new perspective on their relationship – and an incentive when she sees her child developing abilities in talking and playing which she had felt hopeless about. The day-care staff can also monitor how the child progresses, and if there is a deterioration can warn the social worker that things may not be going so well at home. Child minders can do much the same.

Parents may need training in daily child care, home management, household budgeting or other social skills. This applies to fathers as well as mothers. There has been a major change in attitudes to parents sharing care of their children, but some husbands in families where their help is most needed can be the most resistant to change. Again I would stress that seeing how a deprived child can respond to day-centre activities, and begin to talk, play, relate and develop normally, can open parents' eyes to what they have been missing, to what can be done, and motivate them to turn over a new leaf. When there is a long history of inadequacy and neglect, and the parents have their own backgrounds of deprivation, there will be little scope for the starry-eyed worker. But every small goal achieved can be a milestone in helping a family towards independence and self-sufficiency, and often the start has to be made in helping the parents to come to terms with their own problems as individuals, and with problems in their relationship. After that can come their learning how their behaviour has harmed their children, and how to deal with that.

The most difficult assessment of all can be to determine whether a family of neglected children needs to be given a new start, with the disruption and regression that this will be known to cause, in the hope that the right foster placement will give them their best chance in life; or whether months and years of patient endeavour will help the family raise the standards in their own homes and become self-sufficient. The dilemma is whether to replace the parents or supplement their efforts in the hope that they will come to manage.

How can you determine, with assurance, that the apathy and lack of interest shown by parents is irreversible? How many chances do you give them to show a capacity to change, a willingness to better their home conditions, before you give up? It is not the parents' well-being that is the worker's first concern: it is the children's. The task is to try to establish what will be in their best interests, reconciling possibly conflicting priorities in their needs for security, continuity and opportunities to grow and develop.

Family centres for assessment and treatment of chronic inability to cope offer facilities which can be instrumental in resolving such problems; I use the words 'chronic inability' deliberately, because it usually is long-established and deep-seated, although at the time it may often present itself as an acute crisis. These centres are expensive to run and need staff-intensive activity in working with parents, alone and in group activities; with children likewise; and in seeing how families react together and how they can be helped to relate to each other more effectively. When parents and children come into the same room, having been parted temporarily by care arrangements, trained workers can assess what sort of rapport, if any, exists between them, and try to build up their evaluation of the capacity for that relationship to be developed.

Techniques are needed to encourage or deter, using praise, rewards or material help, or by imposing authority in order to make progress. As a GP I sometimes felt ashamed of having used some fairly firm authority on a young couple – until I came to understand that sometimes they *needed* an authoritative figure: they'd never had one, and like their children lacked guidelines on their own behaviour. Perhaps the fact that someone cared enough about them to be angry when they erred gave a security they had never had before.

Who is My Neighbour?

One of the great changes which we have seen in recent years has been the splitting of families; there are many, many young couples trying to learn how to cope with running a home and bringing up their children far away from the support and advice earlier generations would have expected from their own parents. Modern housing arrangements often make it impossible for granny to stay with a family, and while her presence in a home is sometimes regarded as a mixed blessing, so is her absence.

However, in our older – and smaller – communities it was not only the relations – what we now call 'the extended family' – who could advise, help, baby-sit and provide company for a young family; if there were happiness, or trouble, or sickness, it was a neighbourhood concern, and neighbourliness is something which seems to be lacking in some of our communities today, especially in some of the brave new towns, which seem sometimes to be the loneliest places for someone with troubles to be.

There will be those who argue that neighbourly concern is

now exercised more fittingly 'by proxy' – through the professional services provided by the local authorities and health authorities, and by voluntary agencies. This is in one sense true, for there are many circumstances where professional input is necessary. But there are also many occasions when a person, or a couple, or a family, need not a service but a caring friend. This can be a neighbour, a relation, a church visitor; someone who will give a hand with the chores, and perhaps show an inexperienced young mother how to cope with some aspect of housekeeping; a 'granny substitute' who will sit with a sick baby and give mother a much-needed break, or take charge of the children so that a necessary hospital appointment can be kept; someone who might even say, 'Come on, love, you look worn out – why not let my husband and me look after the girls for an evening while you have a hair-do and the two of you have a night out?' Various parents' self-help groups can do marvellous work in much the same way, and even the realisation that there really are other people, who look quite normal, and have the same problems and worries, can be therapeutic in itself. 'You mean that there are others who feel like this? Who get it wrong about their children? Who sometimes feel they can't cope and must be the worst parents ever? That I can talk to and share my feelings with? What a relief!'

Holiday Breaks

When I first started working with the NSPCC I had a fairly low regard for those who placed insistence on providing holidays for children, and sometimes for families. I wondered what such a short break, however enjoyable, could achieve compared with the months of unsatisfactory home life. It did not take me long to realise how very wrong I was.

To a child brought up in some of the deprived conditions I have described, even a few days spent in a clean and lovely place, with fun things to do, plenty of good food and a relaxed though ordered atmosphere could be a revelation that might change their whole attitude to life, and give them to hope that they could break out of the dreadful mesh in which they are caught and build up life of a different quality. After a break relationships within the home can be different and a new start can be made. Those who work so hard to provide holidays for deprived families are good neighbours indeed. And the offer of a holiday can be a very useful incentive to use as part of a 'contract' – a reward that can be offered in response to achieving a clearly defined improvement as part of a mutually agreed treatment plan.

Education Campaigns

It is clear that a great deal of neglect of children is due to ignorance. Parents who have had poor opportunities in their own upbringing can be ignorant and apathetic about their own performance; more often they may start with the right intentions but slowly sink when the going gets hard. Many members of the public may not realise how widespread and insidious a danger neglect can be, and fail to reach out to those in need – and this can apply to professionals, too.

In 1986 the NSPCC set up the most ambitious educational campaign it had ever tried. Its President, Princess Margaret, appeared on television, talking about neglected children as 'the Forgotten Children whom we must not let the world forget'. A public information video was produced, and widely screened. A series of advertisements was placed in newspapers and selected magazines. Posters were placed in stations, at bus stops and other sites where they would be seen. A booklet was produced, for free distribution, which described neglect, how to recognise it and what to do about it. Staff throughout the country raised the topic at professional gatherings, especially the Area Review Committees responsible for coordinating child abuse procedures and arranging training programmes. National conferences were held.

The purpose was to target parents, the public generally and professional workers with the message that neglect exists, is widespread and is a form of child abuse that can be fatal; and that something can be done about it, which needs all of those targeted to be aware of the problem, try to understand it and be prepared to do something. This purpose was certainly achieved in part at least, as market research undertaken before, during and after the campaign showed very definite changes in awareness and attitudes.

Becoming 'Good Enough'

One important precept is to avoid setting one's sights too high. In our concern that each child should have the proper opportunity through the proper standards of parental and home care to develop to its full and unique potential, we can try to convert the inadequate home into a perfect one – and will always fail, because there are no perfect parents, not even you, and certainly not myself!

Most parents provide good enough care for their children, and that should be the aim when neglect is found. The question to be asked is, is there scope for improvement or are attitudes so intractable that it is not worth trying? Or, as in the great majority of instances, is there enough capacity for change to try to bring standards up to the 'good enough' – even though it may sometimes be only just good enough? 'Only just good enough' may seem an over-modest ambition, but it may be the most realistic one in helping children to have the security of staying within their own family, and of having their own sights raised so that as they mature they can work for themselves at the 'only just' part.

In 1987, of 23,000 cases referred to the NSPCC because of a suspicions of child abuse, over 10,000 related to neglect, failure to thrive, or being left alone. These are not minor problems. They are often very intractable ones, particularly as parents who are neglectful seem to be less ready than any other category to accept that things are not right, or to be prepared or able to do something about it. Better training of parents and professionals, and above all better routine surveillance of young children, are essential if thousands of lives are not to be blighted every year.

Chapter Five: **Physical Abuse**

Physical abuse, the 'non-accidental injury' of children, is the form of child cruelty which first comes to mind when the subject is mentioned. Physical injuries are – largely – visible; their existence is demonstrable evidence of pain and suffering, which when deliberately caused evoke immediate sympathy with the victim and outrage about the perpetrator.

Physical abuse is the most common recorded cause of child cruelty deaths, which, as we have seen, number some three or four a week, according to the best estimates we can make. Approximately 10,000 cases of physical abuse are discovered each year of a severity that warrants placing the children's names upon child abuse registers; how many further cases occur which are not detected, or are of lesser severity, is not known, but there must be at least as many, not taking into account the perennial question of 'excessive chastisement' whether deliberate or unintended.

An eight-year-old boy called Peter Betts was placed on a child abuse register after the social services had investigated an incident in which he had been beaten with a belt resulting in a badly bruised bottom and back. The NSPCC was asked to take on the management of the case. Mr Betts admitted to the beating, and explained that it happened because he had lost his temper with the boy, who had given a toy to one of his friends without asking permission.

Mr and Mrs Betts confessed to severe marital problems; they had parted company on a number of occasions. In the course of a series of interviews they began to understand how their troubled relationship was affecting their children, of whom Peter was the oldest. His behaviour was undoubtedly causing problems at school, as well as at home, and his father could see no way of controlling him other than by hitting him.

Peter's father had himself been abused as a child, and he needed to be helped to understand that his own children were misbehaving because of the strains within the home which he and his wife were causing; Peter was reacting to the unhappiness he felt – and was therefore being punished (and excessively punished) as, in effect, a scapegoat. Both parents came to understand how their own relationship problems were having an adverse effect on their family, and the father was helped to come to terms with his own past experience; he was taught to use ways of disciplining Peter without having to hit him.

Unfortunately, despite improvements in Peter's behaviour and in his parents' understanding, the parents' relationship deteriorated and the family split up, but this case demonstrates how many cases of physical injury to children begin because of distorted views on how to discipline children. It also shows an underlying failure to realise the reason for their misbehaviour, and that no amount of punishment will change it; indeed, a child frightened of losing his parents' love may cultivate behaviour that causes punishment – he's being noticed, and feels he still matters enough to get attention, however painful.

The Identification of Physical Abuse

Fig. 10 shows the range and comparative incidence of different types of injuries sustained by children in the NSPCC research series. It will be apparent straight away that establishing that a child has been physically abused is often far from being an easy or straightforward process. There are some injuries which can conclusively be diagnosed as deliberately inflicted but many more cannot. While in general terms it may be better to be a little too suspicious of an injury being non-accidental than let it pass as a result of not being on the look-out for child cruelty, the great trauma and unhappiness

	1982	
Serious head injuries		
Skull fractures	21	(2.6)*
Subdural haematoma	6	(0.7)
Retinal haemorrhage	9	(1.1)
Other brain damage	3	(0.4)
Two or more serious head injuries	8	(1.0)
Other fractures		
Long bone	31	(3.8)
Others	21	(2.6)
Two or more fractures	14	(1.7)
Soft tissue injuries (STI)		
Bruising/welts (head/face)	355	(44.0)
Bruising/welts (body/limbs)	386	(47.8)
Laceration (head/face)	59	(7.3)
Laceration (boby/limbs)	38	(4.7)
Burn, scald	49	(8.1)
Other injuries		
Attempted strangulation/ drowning/suffocation	7	(0.9)
Ingestion	4	(0.5)
Concussion/convulsions	1	(0.1)
Others	11	(1.4)

* Bracketed figures show percentage of cases with this injury. As several cases have more than one injury, the total of these figures exceeds 100.

FIG. 10 NATURE OF ABUSE SUSTAINED 1987

that can result from wrongful accusations must always be borne in mind.

One cannot make an assessment of the injury without other information, apart from the injury itself, much of which will be obtained from the story of how the injury happened, and sometimes from how it was dealt with. Also, more examination may be required. In 1963 two British doctors named Griffiths and Moynihan published an article in the *British Medical Journal* (see p. 82) in which they described X-ray findings of bone injuries that were part of the 'battered baby syndrome', as it came to be called at that time, stressing the importance of X-ray examination – and warning doctors not to be 'reluctant to believe that such assaults on innocent babies are possible'. If there are bruises or other signs of

injuries that have been deliberately inflicted, X-ray examination is essential in case there are hidden bone injuries as
well – and this applies in cases of suspected neglect also.

When looking for additional information while assessing a
case of physical injury, it is worth asking the following
questions.

Is the child showing other signs of abuse? We have already
looked at the need to have X-ray examination when child
abuse is suspected. It must also be recognised that human
behaviour does not always fit into neat categories. Different
forms of abuse and neglect can occur in the same family or
can be seen in the same child, and they should be looked for.

Is the nature of the injury consistent with the age of the child? A
bruise which might very naturally happen to a toddler falling
and banging into some hard object should be looked at very
suspiciously if it is found on a baby that is too young to walk
or even crawl.

Does the explanation make sense? A boy with bad bruising on
both buttocks was said to have hurt himself by 'running
backwards into a fence' – how? A child with badly blistered
feet was said to have 'stepped into a bath that was too hot,
doctor'. Could she really have placed one foot into boiling hot
water – and then the other (and only scalded the tops of her
feet)?

Are there too many explanations (or none)? A social worker or a
doctor may feel nonplussed when very definite signs of injury
are commented on by a parent as though they hadn't
happened; it can be equally disturbing to find that the story
changes each time that it is told – which is an additional
reason for sharing information, because unless different
people realise that they are being given different explanations
their suspicions may not be aroused.

Has the parent acted promptly to get the right treatment? One of
the worries of those of us whose work lies in dealing with
child abuse is that the over-reaction that can come from the
media reporting of incidents such as the Cleveland Sexual
Abuse scandal of 1987 can inhibit parents from taking injured
children to the doctor, lest they be accused of abuse and have
their children wrested from them before they can do a thing

about it. Normally, an inexplicable delay in bringing an injured child for medical attention should cause suspicion that the matter is not a straightforward one.

Finally, *is there, or has there been, other abuse?* This question should apply to the child who now has injuries, and to any others in the household. Sometimes there may be a plausible explanation for a child to have bruising, but when it happens again the excuse begins to look less convincing. One of the other reasons for the need to make extensive enquiries within the professional network is that other workers may have records of similar injuries affecting other children in the family. When three successive children in a family have similar unexplained head injuries on three successive occasions it is time to have a careful review.

Suspicion of abuse, therefore, needs very careful evaluation of the story and of the history of the family, and methodical examination of the child – not just of the injury that is presented. But what are the injuries that are being looked for, and how can you tell that they are not accidental? Certainly any anxious parent can get in a muddle and tell a story that doesn't seem to fit the circumstances, but it is often hard to tell whether this is indeed so, or whether the facts are more complex, as in the following case of the Davis family.

A situation came to light in the west country when Stephen, aged three, was taken to the casualty department by his aunt. His left arm was broken. His mother, Susan, aged twenty-two, denied any knowledge of how it could have happened. She said that she had only noticed it on the morning that Stephen was taken to hospital but she had no explanation for the delay between the time she agreed that she had noticed the injury and the time at which Stephen had been taken to the hospital.

Susan was questioned further by a paediatrician and after a conversation at the hospital with the child's father, Peter, aged twenty-eight, the parents said that the injury had in fact occurred the evening before and that they had been aware of it. Peter is a very strong man who enjoys weight-lifting. He said that the injury must have been caused when he was lifting Stephen out of his pushchair.

The family were living with Susan's sister and on the evening in question Peter baby-sat for the women whilst they visited the cinema. The child had been left, strapped into his pushchair, when they went out and had subsequently cried. Peter had decided to give him comfort and went to lift him from the chair. Whilst doing so he burnt himself on a radiator and failed to notice that Stephen was strapped in and had jerked the child. He told his wife what had happened and the following morning they had both noticed that Stephen's arm was swollen. Neither could explain why they had not gone to the hospital sooner. Further full examinations were carried out and Stephen was found to have a healing burn on his left foot, some three weeks older than the fracture of his arm. There was also old bruising on his back. Subsequently, when an X-ray examination was carried out, further fractures were found to be present in his leg in addition to the greenstick fracture seen in his arm.

An investigation was carried out and it emerged that in addition to these violent injuries there was a high degree of neglect. The child had been badly cut by a bottle; the cuts had been infected but Susan had not taken him to the doctor nor to the clinic. Susan was in an advanced stage of pregnancy at the time and had a very poor record of attendance at the clinic. She appeared to take very little, if any, care for herself. Shortly after these events came to light she gave birth to twins who were six weeks premature.

As workers got to know the family better a very bizarre picture emerged. Susan's sister, who had much of the care of Stephen, was herself ill with chronic asthma. Both the sisters were very hostile towards authority, having been brought up in an extremely deprived family. Susan's sister had herself had a child at the time that Stephen was born but the baby had died shortly after birth. Peter spent most of the day at a local gym and seemed to have no inclination to look for employment although he was able and had reasonable qualifications acquired whilst at school.

In this case Stephen was voluntarily placed in care for a period but in time returned home. Susan was allowed to keep the other children and received help from the NSPCC for several years. Peter admitted that he had broken Stephen's arm in temper and was subsequently prosecuted and received a six-month prison sentence. The family responded to social work support.

In this case we became aware of multiple fractures of different ages, bruising, a burn and a cut, made worse by neglect. It might be helpful to look at some common injuries found to have been inflicted on children.

The Torn Frenulum

If you push the tip of your tongue up behind your top lip you will feel a tiny ridge of skin between the lip and the top of the gum: this is the frenulum. This can be torn or ruptured, which is almost invariably by a deliberate act – either a blow to the mouth, or a savage thrust on a feeding bottle. It is often associated with a parent's misplaced anger when there is a feeding difficulty; 'misplaced' because baby cannot explain what is wrong, and the parent doesn't know what to do and gets ill-tempered. Injuries like this in the mouth heal very quickly, and therefore need to be looked for immediately.

Black Eyes

'Two lovely black eyes' go the words of the song – and the reason for them was two deliberate punches. The same goes for injuries to children, for it is practically impossible to have both eyes blacked by one injury, unless there is other major damage to the bones of the upper face, such as the orbit of the eye. Consequently the explanation 'he fell from his cot' or 'she fell downstairs' should be met with immediate suspicion and further enquiry. When did it happen? Who was there, and what were they doing? Could a child of that age have fallen in that way unaided? How long ago did it happen? 'We came round straight away' may not fit with bruising which from its colouring is obviously several days old – or which indeed may look as though there are different bruises inflicted on separate occasions.

Nor does it have to be both eyes that are black for the story to be suspect. If a child falls the tendency will be for the prominent bony parts of the face to be injured, and for the soft tissues in the hollows between them to be protected from harm. It takes something rounded, such as a fist, to get between the cheekbone, nose and the forehead and black the eye.

Soft Tissue Bruising
Similarly, a variety of injuries that are caused deliberately will be found on parts of the body that are normally protected from accidental damage: bruising inside the ear, on the inner aspects of the thighs and around the genitals (sometimes associated with sexual abuse, but often related to 'punishment' for bedwetting). Bruises of different ages can often be seen on lively youngsters when they are out at play and up to mischief day after day; but the injuries should be consistent with the stories, and with the activities described – the bumps and scrapes sustained when playing football are very different in the distribution on the body from some of the serious and unusual injuries which abusing parents claim are due to playing games. It is rare for a baby to be bruised accidentally, until it is old and mobile enough to be capable of causing accidents of its own making.

Finger Bruising
Harsh gripping by adult fingers and thumbs can result in distinct finger bruising. This can be associated with punitive pinching of the face, or gripping the upper arms or body and shaking a child – or, more horrifyingly, when a child is picked up by its lower limbs and viciously swung like a club at grave risk to its life, depending on what its head should strike against.

Bite Marks
Another sign that is diagnostic of deliberate abuse is the human bite mark, and the story 'It must have been one of the other children' can usually be discounted by the size of the bite. Classically there will be two semicircles of bruising with a gap between them on either side. There may be further bruising within the circle, but often there the skin is unmarked. Some teeth may have punctured the skin, and as

the bruising fades the marks of individual teeth sometimes become more apparent. These bites can occur almost anywhere on the body – face, torso, arms, legs or even the genitalia. Blows with the open hand also cause finger and hand bruising, but – unlike the blows with a stick or cane – do not raise weals.

Burns
Plate 4 shows a burn that could hardly be described as having occurred naturally. This boy's bare bottom had been deliberately and firmly pressed against a hot electric cooking ring. There are many instances of burns which more or less clearly show the shape of the heated object that has been pressed against the child's flesh – a poker, a key, an iron.

In a class of their own are cigarette burns (plate 2), which seem to be a common means of punishment, or torture. If a child gets accidentally burned by a lighted cigarette, this is likely to be from brushing against it; fragments of lighted tobacco may adhere to the skin and cause several small burn marks along the line of the movement that occurred. This appearance will be quite different from the small neat circular burn that happens when a lighted cigarette is deliberately held against a child's face or body. What is more, a child who accidentally gets a burn from touching a lighted cigarette is likely to be cautious about getting another; inflicted burns can often be seen to be multiple, across the face and chest for example, and to have happened on different occasions, with some fresh, others at various stages of healing.

Scalds
I have referred to the scalded feet that come from being placed in boiling water, and to the discrepancy in the story. What child, old and lively enough to clamber into the bath, would not be wary of steaming hot water – and put one foot into scalding water after the other? A much feared accident to children is when they pull a kettle or saucepan off the cooker and scald themselves. When this happens, and is a genuine accident, questions have to be asked about any degree of negligence, in leaving a child alone in the kitchen, letting

saucepan handles stick out within reach and so on. When there is doubt, more questions need to be considered. Was the child capable of reaching up in the way described? Is the distribution of the scald marks consistent with the story, or are they on parts of the body that just do not fit what was said to have happened? Was scalding hot liquid deliberately used as a punishment?

X-ray Evidence

I cannot stress too much the importance of X-ray evidence when there is suspicion of child abuse. This does not only apply to suspected physical injury, for, as the late Dr Christine Cooper pointed out, some 17 per cent of children reported to her in Newcastle for neglect were found – on full medical examination including radiology – to have physical injuries as well.

About five years ago I was told of a baby that had been admitted to hospital with bronchopneumonia; despite treatment she had died, and a doctor who was rather suspicious of the 'feel' of the whole case ordered post-mortem X-rays of the whole body. Sure enough the X-rays showed a series of fractures, some recent, some at different stages of healing, of practically every major – 'long' – bone in her arms and legs. Multiple rib fractures were the cause of the bronchopneumonia that appeared to have killed her: the true cause of death was murder.

While there had been a few reports in specialist medical journals before then, in the *British Medical Journal* of 21 December 1963 Drs Griffiths and Moynihan published a classic paper, the first of its kind, entitled 'Multiple Epiphysial Injuries in Babies ('Battered Baby Syndrome')'. In it they wrote:

> We hope in this paper to give publicity to a syndrome which we think commoner than is usually believed, and which would appear often to be misdiagnosed, with possibly tragic results. It concerns babies brought to hospital with unexplained swellings in the region of the ends of long bones who are in fact victims of unsuspected trauma which is often brutal and which has usually been inflicted by a parent.
>
> The patients we report were all under one year old, but the

literature contains accounts of the same thing in older children. An essential feature of the syndrome is that the history of trauma is not forthcoming, for it is suppressed by the culprit, while the victim is too young to give a history at all. This absence of history, or the substitution of a misleading or untrue history, is one reason for failure to make the correct diagnosis.

In these few words these two wise and experienced orthopaedic surgeons have encapsulated much that is fundamental to today's child abuse practice. When children are brought, probably rather belatedly, to hospital with unexplained injuries, or with a bizarre or misleading story, the diagnosis of abuse can be missed – unless the nurse or doctor is alert. This was another point made by these pioneers in the same article: having described the 'real risk' of further and more serious, or even fatal, injury in such cases, they went on to say that it is a doctor's duty not only to recognise the syndrome but also to report cases to the police, for:

> We cannot return children to parents in whose care they may have a 10 per cent chance of violent death. Doctors are reluctant to believe that such assaults on innocent babies are possible, and they are even more reluctant to become involved in the squalor of criminal proceedings, but in the interests of some of our most helpless patients we must realise that epiphysial trauma [bone damage of a particular nature] is due to violence and that not all parents, even if warned, are safe custodians.

In the days when I was a medical student, a decade before this paper appeared, there was a terrifying ignorance. I can remember being under instruction at the Belgrave Hospital for Children, an historic place near London's Oval reduced now to an empty hulk, when an uninspiring mother produced her child, a pallid silent girl of six or seven, saying that she had 'hit her arm against a car'. This sounded a very unlikely story. The submissive girl had nothing else to say, and when mother was asked to undress her for examination and ripped her coat off in a way that might have caused any child distress, and there was no complaint, we looked at each other – and wondered. Was this a cock-and-bull story, with no real injury? Surely a really injured child would have cried out? (We had not the wit to understand the reality of what was happening.) To our amazement, the X-ray showed a distinct spiral fracture of the humerus – the long bone of the upper arm.

Those were the innocent days, when doctors, hearing an unlikely story, thought 'How odd!' and went on with treating the specific injury. I often look back upon that incident and wonder what would have happened in these hopefully more enlightened days? Would we have thought to ourselves 'Is this a natural injury?' – for we should have done. Would we have alerted the GP, the health visitor, the Social Services Department, as to our suspicions? In those days, I am sure that we would not have even dreamed of such action. Yet, in all probability, we had been confronted with a case of wilful cruelty to a child – and had failed that child.

I have mentioned some of the externally visible injuries which may lead to suspicion of their being non-accidental in origin. Among these are bruising and haemorrhage, in the superficial layers of the skin, which may be caused by hands, thumbs or fingers, or by a variety of implements – straps, sticks, wires, belts, and every domestic implement from a shoe to a hairbrush. There is a variety of bruising (which comprises an area where blood has exuded from a damaged blood vessel and invaded the skin and underlying tissue) known as petechial haemorrhage. Petechiae are minute separate spots of blood which have been forced out of individual minuscule capillary blood vessels, with the appearance of a very fine rash; one can sometimes see them within the circle of toothmarks in a bite mark, and they can show as superficial damage accompanied by deeper bruising after, say, a beating. Bruises change colour and slowly fade as the blood is chemically broken down and absorbed by the body's defence system; one can see that some bruises may be older than others, but it is not possible to be precise about this process.

However, there are other forms of haemorrhage which can result from internal injuries, accidental or non-accidental, and which will not be visible on external inspection. When a bone is cracked or broken, or 'bruised', there can sometimes be considerable internal bleeding; this may in time show through the skin, possibly at some distance from the injury, as the blood exudes between layers of tissue. There can be haemorrhage within muscles and inside body cavities; if some internal organ like the spleen is damaged by a heavy blow the haemorrhage can reach fatal proportions without there being any external sign of blood loss. In such cases diagnosis of physical abuse may depend upon the circumstances, rather than the nature of the damage; if a cot-bound baby has severe internal abdominal injuries for which there is no plausible explanation, the presumption will be a deliberate blow.

The other important thing to consider is the possibility of haemorrhage within the brainbox. This can be bleeding within the substance of the brain, with resultant brain damage, or it can be bleeding from the vessels in the coverings of the brain; as the brainbox or cranium is rigid, the pressure of blood flowing out between the soft brain tissue and the hard bone will cause the brain to be compressed and damaged in that way, unless immediate steps are taken to let the blood out – to 'decompress' the brain.

I have mentioned the finger bruising which can result from a child's legs being gripped hard as it is swung, in a bizarre form of violence, with risk of head injury from any hard object that is in the way. The mere pressure of the swinging (or of vigorously shaking a child so that the head moves violently to and fro) can lead to bleeding in the brain coverings – sub-dural haemorrhage – which can be fatal, or can result in varying degrees of physical or mental handicap, akin to the damage from a stroke. Estimates vary but a significant number of children with permanent disability due to brain damage are the victims of physical abuse in such a way.

Brittle Bones
Amongst the hazards of diagnosing non-accidental injury of children, a recent development has been an upsurge of news coverage of the 'brittle bones' syndrome, with allegations that many parents are being unjustly accused of causing multiple

fractures to their babies, when these babies are in fact suffering from a condition where such fractures are inevitable, and which should not be confused with injuries due to child abuse.

That false accusations on so serious a matter should be avoided does not need any emphasis from me. Great distress can be caused to innocent people; families can have their lives disrupted in a way that is of benefit to nobody – least of all the children. On a wider front, the whole cause of preventing cruelty to children can be set back, because its advocates can be discredited. There are plenty of people ready to do this. Writing in *The Independent* in November 1987 Yvonne Roberts referred to newspaper allegations of scandal: 'the scandal being the parents who claim they have been falsely accused. The abused children have been spirited away, their voice unheard, a necessary sacrifice if the good name of the family is to be salvaged.'

Later in the same article she mentions a Member of Parliament who 'refuses to accept widespread sexual abuse as a possibility because the consequences are unthinkable: an *Alice in Wonderland* logic . . . "It can't be happening to you because we say it isn't".' From time to time the NSPCC has been accused of dreaming up child abuse data just to justify its existence, by people with the same unwillingness to face reality.

This is where a proper balance must be struck. If we are to be vigilant for signs of child abuse and neglect, then the possibility must be borne in mind whenever children are seen with injuries or debilities that do not seem to have a natural explanation; this means that sometimes suspicion may be aroused when it is in fact not justified. An NSPCC opinion poll showed a wide public acceptance that this may be unavoidable. On the other hand it would be negligent for child abuse workers to take proceedings for bone injuries being caused to a child if the diagnosis of brittle bone disease is a likely alternative and has not been excluded.

In a leading article in the *British Medical Journal* of 31 October 1987, Dr Taitz, a paediatrician in Sheffield, referred to the need to avoid confusion in the diagnosis of unexplained fractures in babies. In reviewing the various forms of Osteogenesis imperfecta, which is the formal name for brittle bone disease, he points out that in most cases there can be no reason for confusion, except in one form of the disease (Type IV) which is so rare that in a city the size of Sheffield there might be one case every 100 to 300 years, compared with about 15 cases a year of fractures due to non-accidental injury. Dr Taitz concludes by saying that, provided care is taken, brittle bone disease 'does not provide a satisfactory reason for unexplained fractures in otherwise healthy babies'.

We can see that the types of injury which can be deliberately inflicted upon a child (or deliberately allowed to happen through wilful refusal to protect the child) can vary from the excessive use of force to unexpected excessive effects of force. These injuries might occur in circumstances which are understandable, such as a display of anger by a parent. This is not to excuse the act; and some anger may be totally disproportionate to whatever the child has been up to. However, it can be easier to understand how such injuries happen than cases of some deliberate and wilful cruelty, such as forcing a lighted cigarette repeatedly against a child's skin in a sensitive area like the cheek or the genitalia.

A typical case of a parent inflicting physical injury on a child in a display of anger is that of the Blake family. An NSPCC Duty Officer in the Potteries received a call at 11 p.m. on a Friday night from Mrs Blake. She was sobbing and said that she had rung because she was frightened of what her husband might do to their four-year-old girl Patricia. She told me that the previous night her husband had lost his temper when Patricia had been getting ready for bed. Apparently she had not undressed quickly enough for his liking and because she had begun crying he had stuffed a towel into her mouth to stop her screaming. One of Patricia's teeth had been loosened and bled as a result. Then he had thrown Patricia on the floor and she had bruised her back.

She went on to say that about three months previously her husband had lost his temper and hit Patricia hard on her legs, leaving her badly bruised. Her husband worked very long hours because of his work and was often in a bad mood when he came home.

After her husband had lost his temper on the Friday they had both talked over their fears and had agreed to contact the NSPCC. The Inspector visited the family and Mr Blake admitted that he had thrown his daughter on the floor but he couldn't understand why he had lost his temper and had regretted the incident afterwards. He emphasised that he and his wife were very fond of their two children and he did not want to see Patricia or her younger brother who was two years old removed from them. He wanted an assurance that this would not need to happen. He said that rather than the children leave home he would leave and allow his wife to continue to care for the children.

A paediatrician at the local hospital examined the children and confirmed that there were no serious after-effects from Mr Blake's attack on his daughter and no evidence that Patricia's younger brother had been abused. The injury to the inside of Patricia's mouth suggested that Mr Blake had used considerable force.

The Inspector made further visits to the parents and discussed their worries and difficulties with them. Mr Blake's long working hours had placed the family under considerable stress and sometimes he was away for days at a time; they were also experiencing serious financial difficulties. Mrs Blake did not like her husband working such long hours and felt that he was avoiding sharing the responsibility of looking after the children. She also said that she felt lonely and frightened when she was left alone. Mrs Blake thought that her husband was too strict with the children while he felt that she let them get away with anything and that the children took advantage.

At a case conference it was decided to put Patricia's name on the child abuse register. In view of Mr and Mrs Blake's recognition of the problems they faced and their willingness to accept help in overcoming them it was decided that Patricia would not be at risk if she lived at home with both her parents. Working in collaboration with a social worker from the local authority the Inspector designed a programme to help the family resolve their problems in their relationship with each other and in their relationship with Patricia. As the therapeutic programme started, there was every hope that with help the family would be able to overcome their difficulties and that Patricia would not be at risk of further abuse.

I hope that I have shown sufficient examples to demonstrate that there exists a range of injuries which we know parents inflict upon their children and that I have indicated circumstances which should justify a degree of suspicion. The confirmation of suspicions about abuse is a medical matter and it is important for the victim that a comprehensive examination takes place which will extend beyond the superficial and evident injuries. The medical examination must be complemented by a social assessment undertaken by a social worker and enquiries will look for links to other forms of cruelty, such as neglect which we have considered and emotional abuse which is addressed in the following chapters.

Mrs Virginia Bottomley, M.P., has a Bill before Parliament which will, I hope, lead to an improvement in the law. Her purpose is to provide for parents to have to present their children for medical examination if so ordered – without having to lose their parental rights and responsibilities.

Chapter Six: **Sexual Abuse**

Mrs White was a divorcee who lived with her four-year-old daughter Heather in a coastal town. Mr White was allowed to see the child once a week. One day when Heather was in the bathroom with her mother, she tried to push her finger into Mrs White's anus.

'Darling, that is *not* a nice thing to do – and it hurt Mummy!' she said.

'Well, that is what Daddy keeps doing to me,' said Heather. Mother called the NSPCC.

To start the investigation, the Inspector visited and tried to get a clear statement from Mrs White; she explained that Heather had revealed her story suggestive of sexual abuse without using words, and that it seemed to have started when Mr White had taken the child away for a holiday. The police were called, and a medical examination was arranged for the child, who was then professionally interviewed by the NSPCC officer and a policewoman. The doctor had already found evidence of penetration of the girl's anus, and as she had already got to know both the people interviewing her Heather was able to relax and trust them enough to tell her story.

Sexual abuse had been going on for some time, and the little girl was very disturbed, one sign of the trauma she had suffered being frequent nightmares. It was very necessary to develop her confidence in the team of workers, to let her tell her story in her own way and to help her to feel better about herself. Through play and art therapy, Heather began to understand better and to work through the trauma she had suffered. Young children with limited vocabularies can often portray their feelings better with pictures than with words, and this was so with Heather: her paintings showed many figures of an angry monster, and then of a fairy queen who rescued her. Slowly her nightmares stopped.

It was some months before Mr White appeared in court. It was felt that Heather was too young to give evidence, and that after all the progress that she had made in getting over her experiences, it would only compound the abuse that had already happened and bring back all her nightmares and unhappiness if she were subjected to the experience of being brought into court to testify. The medical evidence was not considered sufficient to justify a conviction, so Heather's father was found not guilty and discharged.

There are many points about this case that are important.

The wrong-doer was not a stranger, it was Daddy.

The story only came to light through a seemingly casual act, which might not have been responded to.

Mother was alert to the implications, believed her daughter and acted.

This was not 'normal' intercourse, with a pubescent girl being used as a surrogate wife: the sort of stereotyped situation, which continues with the assumption that a mother who has had enough of conjugal duty will be party to what is happening – 'It's good for the girl, really, and teaches her what she needs to know in a loving environment'. This was repeated buggery of a very small child by her own father.

She was only four.

She suffered great torment which took skill, love and time to begin to heal – and we do not yet know how it will affect her adult life and relationships.

The multiple crimes committed against her little body went unpunished, because the British judicial system has not moved forward since the Criminal Law Amendment Act of 1885. Her molester went free – free to continue to molest small children without let or hindrance.

Whereas a video-recording, taken under strict legal guidelines, and with due regard for the rights of the accused, might have

made Heather's evidence available without trauma to her, the
months of delay in bringing the case to trial (surely a burden for
any innocent accused as well) meant that if she had been taken
into court as a witness the delay would have meant withholding
effective treatment in a way that could have ensured that her
experiences would have ruined her for life instead of being – we
hope – capable of cure; the experience of giving evidence, in the
view of Professor Meadows in a leading article in the *British
Medical Journal* – had it been admissible – could have been more
abusive and traumatic than the original abuse itself.

And that is only a part of the dilemma. Child sexual abuse is
a very secret, disturbing, ill-understood and extraordinarily
difficult problem. Professionals, let alone the public, can find
it hard to conceive that such abuse can happen; can feel
threatened in their own sexuality and personal security and
wish to avoid the issue; can find it such a difficult matter to
recognise, and respond to. How can you crash into such a
fraught and private area of people's lives, unsure if you have
the facts right or not? Yet how can you not try to respond and
reach out to help and protect a child whom you believe to be
suffering great trauma, and to be at grave risk?

Why is this 'new' epidemic happening? Is it happening? Is
there a sudden upsurge in molestation of children, or is it all
just a scare? With laws and behaviour more relaxed in sexual
matters, is the involvement of children becoming more
common – and more accepted? These are only some of the
torrent of questions raised when the subject is brought up in
almost any audience, and some of them are very difficult to
answer.

We all (or nearly all) have strong taboos about incestuous
relationships, and there is a greater tendency to disbelieve
that there can be sexual abuse within the family than with
any other form of child cruelty. This applies also to professionals, who for years have in the large part been sceptical
about whether molestation occurs.

For if at times it has seemed hard to persuade the world that
child cruelty exists within our communities, all communities,
and at every level in society, that was as nothing compared
with gaining acceptance that there exists sexual abuse of

children. The furtive stranger behind the bushes was one thing, but that parents and other relatives could sexually molest innocent young children in their own homes was quite another. For generations people have refused to believe what was going on around them – did not see it even when the evidence was there before them, because they could not accept that such things could happen, and willed it out of their consciousness.

In 1979, when I took up my present post, an early task was to try to establish a very modest research project, at a teaching hospital, with the aim of establishing the rate of incidence of demonstrable sexual abuse amongst physically injured children brought there for treatment. After extensive discussion with worried government officials, both the Home Office and the Department of Health and Social Security agreed; the Metropolitan Police were prepared to use their discretion about intervening in cases so that the research could take place, and nominated an officer to liaise with the research team. Yet despite strong support from some of their colleagues for the project, there were some consultants who just could not accept the evidence that was shown to them, and rejected the research as 'unethical'.

The time was not yet right – and the attitude within the news media was much the same. The first press conference that I held on the subject of sexual abuse had the response from one television news team that they would not be coming – the producer did not feel that the subject was one that could be aired on television.

However, slowly, since then there has been a revolution. While there has at times been a disquieting element of alarmist sensationalism, there has also been some highly responsible and sensitive reporting. This has been a godsend for literally thousands of children. For years, if some poor child, burdened with guilt and worry, tried to tell some other adult that she was being sexually exploited at home, he or she would be disbelieved, branded a filthy-minded little liar.

Now, things are changing. People know that sexual abuse happens. They understand that while 'stranger danger' has been the popular concept of sexual risk, family and friends more often provide the offenders. When a child says, 'I've got a dreadful secret that I must talk to somebody about,' he or she is likely to be listened to, and believed. Because of this shift in understanding, the last five years have witnessed a steady increase in the numbers of cases coming to light; fewer people refuse to believe that this sort of abuse can happen, more adults pluck up the courage to reveal the trauma they went through as children and had to bear alone, more children develop confidence in coming forward and more children are being helped.

One of the most immediate worries of the upsurge in challenged diagnoses of sexual abuse in Cleveland in 1987 was that children were being traumatised through unnecessary removal from their families, and there was great concern at the effects upon whole families. As I have said, the even greater concern in child abuse circles was that the public reaction could put the clock right back – just when we appeared to be having a breakthrough – making children fearful of coming forward and adults hesitant about responding. The judicial inquiry has yet to publish its report as I write.

There is nothing new about sexual abuse of children. In 1895 the Royal Charter granted to the NSPCC listed 'the corruption of their morals' among the wrongs to children that should be prevented. In 1924 Sir Robert Parr, then the Society's Director, presented a paper to a working party at the Home Office which might almost have been written today (Fig. 11). He said that sexual abuse was not just a matter of molestation of vulnerable children by strangers, but happened also in their homes. He mentioned examples of abuse by fathers, and by a mother; that boys were affected as well as girls; that incest was only one example from a range of sexual acts involving children; and that the children involved were sometimes very young. Perhaps this information was too unpalatable for the times.

Only since 1981 has sexual abuse appeared separately upon any child abuse registers; and it is still not formally recommended for inclusion by the existing DHSS guidelines. In 1981 the Register Research showed 27 cases of sexual abuse; by 1985 this had risen to 222 cases, and in 1986 to 527, suggesting a national incidence of the order of 6,000 cases. As more cases came to light, the pattern began to change. The average age began to come down to well below 10 years old; while girls still predominated, the proportion of boys began to rise to over 20 per cent. In 1985 two cases involved babies under one year old. The range of types of sexual molestation became more apparent.

What became difficult was to establish what the likely rate of abuse might be. Retrospective studies suggested that over 10 per cent of the adult population had suffered some form of sexual abuse when young – but the different calculations were not based upon a common definition. Some surveys have been attacked for being alarmist, but my view is that the interpretations have sometimes been alarmist when commentators have ignored the context. I would not fault the often-quoted 1985 MORI poll (Baker and Duncan); I am sure that its conclusions were validly reached in the context of the questions that were posed. However, some studies related not only to sexual acts but also extended to unpleasant experiences, such as being subjected to foul language, or harassment by indecent exposure, which could certainly be regarded as distressing, but which I would not necessarily include within the concept of child abuse.

An activity that many people cannot accept as happening at all, and that extends into many forms of harmful or upsetting involvement of children, can be very difficult to define in words that will be universally accepted. This difficulty becomes greater if there is dispute as to whether some practices are harmful, for there are those who allege that children enjoy and are not harmed by sexual activities with adults.

The definition of sexual abuse that was devised by Drs Ruth and Henry Kempe is as follows:

> The involvement of dependent, developmentally immature children and adolescents in sexual activities that they do not truly comprehend and to which they are unable to give informed consent or that violate the social taboos of family roles.

Offences by Relatives

A good many offences against girls are committed by relatives. When the father is an offender it does not always follow that it is a case of incest, as the accompanying table will shew. This is another class of case in which detection is difficult.

News-paper Date	Offence	Age of Girl	Relative Offender	Result	Tried by
13/12/19	Rape	15	Step-father	Reduced to a charge of Indecent Assault. 6 mths. H.L.	Justices.
10/1/20	I.A.	13	Father	21 days H.L. Girl taken away.	Justices.
12/1/20	Rape	14	Father	4 years P.S.	Assizes sentence confirmed by Court of Appeal.
3/2/20	Serious	Not given	Uncle	Acquitted	Quarter Sessions.
28/2/20	C.K.	13	Cousin	2 years H.L.	Assizes.
2/3/20	Incest	Not given	Father	5 yrs. P.S.	Assizes.
20/3/20	I.A.	14	Step-father	6 mths.	Justices.
29/12/20	Brothel-keeping	14 and boy of 13.	Mother (French woman)	Fined £20 and £10 10s. costs—Deportation Order.	Stipendiary.
27/1/21	Incest	13	Father	3 yrs. P.S.	Assizes.
28/1/21	C.K.	14 (girl had child)	Uncle	9 mths. H.L.	Assizes.
7/7/22	Serious	Young	Brother	6 mths.	Assizes.
16/7/22	Attempted C.K.	14	Step-father	12 mths. H.L.	Assizes.
3/8/22	I.A.	14 and 10	Father	18 mths. H.L.	Assizes.
3/9/22	C.K.	15 and 13	Step-father	Certified unfit to plead. To be detained during His Majesty's pleasure.	Assizes.
28/10/22	Incest	Not given	Father	5 yrs.	Central Criminal Court.
16/12/22	I.A.	10	Father	1 mth. H.L.	Justices.
9/7/24	I.A.	15	Uncle	2 mths H.L.	Justices.
–/4/24	I.A.	15 and 13	Father	6 mths. on each charge	Justices.
23/8/24	I.A.	2–young	Uncle	4 mths. H.L.	Justices.
29/8/24	I.A.	12	Father	6 mths. H.L. Child taken away.	Stipendiary.
15/9/24	I.A.	9 and 10	Father	6 mths. each offence, consecutive.	Justices.
24/10/24	Incest	Young	Father	Convicted for I.A., 3 mths.	Assizes
28/10/24	C.K.	15 and 12	Uncle	6 mths. H.L.	Assizes.
3/11/24	I.A.	Young	Grandfather	6 mths.	Justices.

News-paper Date	Offence	Age of Girl	Relative Offender	Result	Tried by
7/11/24	Incest	3, all under 14.	Father	Not guilty on one charge–3 yrs. P.S. and 12 mths. imprison-ment, con-current.	Assizes.
11/11/24	C.K.	13–girl pregnant	Step-father	2 yrs. H.L., child taken away	Assizes.
15/11/24	Incest	17 and 14	Father	7 yrs. P.S.	Assizes.
6/12/24	Incest	Young	*Father	3 yrs. P.S.	Assizes.
13/12/24	C.K. (man charged on nine counts).	2–young	Step-father to one girl.	10 yrs. P.S.	Assizes.
–/1/25	I.A.	8	Grandfather, aged 70.	No prosecution (lack of corr.). Girl placed in Home.	
11/2/25	I.A.	Young	Uncle	3 mths.	Justices.
15/2/25	Incest	15	Father	7 yrs. P.S.	Assizes.
22/2/25	Incest	11 and 7, and boy 9	Brother, aged 18	4 yrs. P.S.	Assizes.

Fig. 11 EXTRACT FROM NSPCC OCCASIONAL PAPER, 1924,
ROBERT J. PARR, OBE

and the staff of the NSPCC use a variant in the following terms:

Children under seventeen years who are involved in sexual acts with a parent or care-giver to which they are unable to give informed consent because of dependence or developmental immaturity, and which are against the law.

One of the most significant terms in each of these definitions is 'informed consent'. There are those who say that sexual involvement of children is often 'with their consent', but if a little girl of four, or a boy of seven, says 'Yes, I like doing this,' do they really know what they are saying? Are they aware of the psychological impact, the physical harm, the risk of disease, of sexual activities which they do not understand. If to have Daddy's (or Mummy's, or uncle's) love and attention means accepting doing funny and sometimes painful things, then yes, anyone with sufficiently twisted a mind could say that there was consent. But it could not be *informed* consent. It would be true to say that an adult relative who claims to have obtained 'consent' has been guilty of an abuse of power, of making unfair use of the natural authority of their relationship.

When one considers the forms that sexual abuse may take it becomes more difficult to accept that consent was willing; silence has persisted so long that what really happens is not appreciated, and it is necessary to be explicit about the range of abusive acts, because the truth needs to be known, and faced up to, if proper action is to be taken. Features of child sexual abuse include:

> Intercourse, anal or vaginal. (Anal intercourse, or buggery, is the more common form in children of both sexes under the age of six years.)
>
> Oral sex.
>
> Masturbation, mutual masturbation, or fondling.
>
> Vaginal/anal penetration by object.
>
> Involvement in sexual activities.
>
> Exposure to pornography – e.g. videos – in the home.
>
> Using children for pornographic purposes.
>
> Child prostitution.

Claims are also made that children do not suffer harm and that a little gentle loving with an erotic content can be mutually enjoyable. In some of the activities outlined above such claims are a little hard to stomach. It may be that it is so with certain children in certain circumstances, but I would always be fearful for the longer-term effects of even seemingly untroubled activities. How do you predict which, if any, children 'will not be harmed'? What an upbringing it must be if a child believes that the only way to gain affection or reward is to offer himself or herself for someone else's sexual gratification.

This can be the very way that a case can come to light. A teacher or other adult may find a child behaving very promiscuously, perhaps making overt sexual advances, because that child's whole experience has been that sex is the basis for securing friendship, kindness and love. (This of course can be a recipe for leaving a child open to further abuse.)

The headmaster of a local school in Lancashire reported a case concerning one of his pupils, an eight-year-old girl called Helen Sampson. There had been a lot of concern about this child, who had been very depressed and showing disturbed behaviour when at school. For some months she had been seeing a psychologist, following an episode when she had tried to throw herself from an upstairs window. Then one of Helen's friends told a teacher that Helen was having sex with her father.

As soon as this was reported the NSPCC visited the school and interviewed Helen with the help of a woman teacher. After a little encouragement Helen disclosed that her father had made her take part in oral sex with him and had made her masturbate him. It was very important to the child to have the reassurance of being believed when she told this story, and the interview was gently brought to an end with further assurance that she was not to blame, and that it was not her fault that these activities had been happening.

This case was discussed with the police. It was decided that Helen should be interviewed again, by the same NSPCC officer together with a medical specialist. She described again, in graphic detail, the nature of the sexual sessions with her father. In bygone days she would probably have been disbelieved and accused of being a lurid liar – but how could a little girl know such details about different acts of sex, and describe them so vividly if she had not been party to them? In fact, with further gentle questioning Helen revealed even more serious problems, for it came out that she was being made to take part in sexual activities by her cousin, a lad of sixteen, and also by two other men who were 'friends of the family'. Mrs Sampson showed very little feeling for her daughter, and it became apparent later that she had had quite specific information about what was being done to Helen and had ignored it.

In these circumstances there was only one thing that could be done to protect this grossly abused little girl: a Place of Safety Order was obtained and she was taken to a children's home. The police were informed of the disclosures Helen had made, and the father and the cousin were taken in for questioning. Both eventually admitted sexual offences and received appropriate custodial sentences when they came to trial. The two 'family friends' were found to be living many miles away; they too were seen by the police, admitted the allegations and went to prison.

So the wicked perpetrators all went to gaol, the little girl was taken in to care and all was well. Or was it? What of Helen's future? She has been conditioned to respond in a sexual way to all the male figures in her life. Simple, innocent contacts, so important to a child, like physical touch, cuddling or showing love, to Helen just mean sex. The task of restoring her innocence, putting the clock back for her, helping her to become a child again, is a virtually impossible one. Her future is most uncertain.

We do not always know how best to help children who have been so abused – indeed, we need to be very careful that in 'putting things right' from an adult's viewpoint we are not compounding the problem for the person most needful of our help, the child. Putting a molesting father or other relative away in prison may be richly deserved; it may be what the public demands; but sometimes it may be quite the wrong thing to do if we want the child victim to recover from the psychological trauma of sexual abuse.

The pressures upon a victim can be enormous. In seeking the love and approbation of a respected adult, be it parent or other relative or friend, a child may feel a guilty party in accepting sexual activities – part of the 'contract' to be entered into to achieve approbation and reward. Some of the fondling and caressing may indeed be pleasurable, adding to the feeling of shared guilt, of co-responsibility. If the victim is a boy he may show demonstrable sexual arousal and therefore feel partly responsible.

To tell of one's burden may be so necessary in order to get some relief, yet at the same time it can be the cause of further guilt because one has betrayed the trust of someone who should be totally trusted and has broken a promise to keep 'our little secret'. After the relief of disclosure there can come the reaction of guilt, which can be added to by the reactions of the rest of the family.

Mother may have been a willing – or an unwilling, or a wilfully blind – accomplice: keeping the breadwinner in the home and assuring his sexual comfort may be given a higher priority than the peace of mind of one of the children.

After fifteen-year-old Sarah Carter and her young sister Jo, who was thirteen years old, went to their older brother Michael and told him that they had been sexually abused by their father, Michael called the police and the girls were taken to a place of safety. The NSPCC were called in immediately; it took legal proceedings and the girls were made the subject of Interim Care Orders and placed with foster parents.

Their father had been sexually abusing the girls since they were very young – fondling them, using sexually explicit language and committing incest. Their mother had threatened to kill the girls if they told anyone. The mother knew of what was going on but felt unable to get help.

The father eventually admitted his guilt which meant that the children didn't need to go through the harrowing experience of giving evidence in court. He was charged with rape and incest and was jailed for four years.

The emotional scars on the girls were deep – Jo in particular had very low self-esteem and had extreme difficulty in making any kind of relationship. Both were helped by the NSPCC to join a group for sexually abused girls, and the NSPCC also needed to work with the mother to help her face up to her responsibilities.

The girls are making progress slowly but surely, and further therapeutic work with the family is being planned.

The one who 'splits on Dad' may be very unpopular with all of the rest of the family; there are frequent instances of children who retract their allegations, which must often be a reflection of family pressures which make the victim feel the guilty party. In such cases, what hope then is there of cure, or even relief?

Melinda Milton, aged eleven years, ran away from her home in Essex and went to stay with her uncle and aunt. She told them that her father had been sexually abusing her. The police and Social Services Department were informed immediately and the Social Services Department took out a Place of Safety Order to protect Melinda. Melinda was subsequently placed in a children's home. The police interviewed Melinda's father, but he denied sexually abusing her and was supported in his denial by his wife. The NSPCC were called in and asked by the local Social Services Department to attend the initial case conference. It was decided at the case conference that the Social Services Department would bring the matter before the juvenile court.

Following a visit to her older brother and his wife, Melinda retracted her allegations. A further case conference was held at which it was decided that Melinda would remain in the children's home and that the NSPCC would try to work with the family to understand what had happened and why Melinda had changed her story. The NSPCC team members who were involved with the family had a strong suspicion that Melinda had been pressurised by her relatives into changing her story. When the parents were interviewed by the NSPCC they continued to deny that Melinda had been sexually abused. However, when the case was heard by the juvenile court Melinda was made the subject of a Care Order.

Mr. and Mrs Milton have since separated and are now getting a divorce. Following the separation Melinda's mother acknowledged that the abuse had happened and expressed to Melinda her deep regret for not protecting her daughter. The NSPCC are working towards rehabilitating Melinda with her mother, but at this point it is not known whether this will be possible.

For those who wish to study this subject further, David Finkelhor and his associates have produced an authoritative and sensitive book entitled *A Sourcebook on Child Sexual Abuse* (Sage, 1986). In a helpful analysis of the problems affecting the child, they suggest four traumatising factors:

1. *Traumatic sexualisation* of the child, whose emergent or dormant sexuality is forced abruptly into an inappropriate stage of development, and of relationship.

2. *Stigmatisation*, whereby the child's own perceptions of self become damaged, with feelings of being soiled and degraded.

3. *Betrayal:* someone on whom the child was dependent, and who was trusted, has abused that trust.

4. *Powerlessness*: the child feels helpless to influence events whatever her or his wishes or desires or sense of what ought to be.

The effects of these all interact, of course, but it is helpful to have a framework upon which to begin to understand the problems that beset an abused child, although I agree with Finkelhor that it may take years of careful study before we can really begin to understand the effects – and the causes – of child sexual abuse.

It is understandable that some children can respond by developing an increasing sexual promiscuity: when they are younger it may be because they have been conditioned to think that this is how to act, and when they are a little older there can be an element of perversity, when the pain and outrage that are felt lead to behaviour that is deliberately outrageous to others. One can understand the findings, in Australia,[1] of sexually abused children being much more prone to commit crimes of violence – as if they are revenging themselves for the stigmatisation they have had to endure. One can see how they may have difficulty in coming to terms with normal relationships – indeed how they may work through their feelings of betrayal by betraying others – for many sexual abusers seem to come from the ranks of the previously abused.

And what of the abuser? How can anybody treat a child in such a way? This again is an area where we know little, and where each new theory is likely to be seized upon, and perhaps given undue weight, as we try to grapple with something so obscene, so threatening to any sense of decency,

[1] *The Persisting Effects of Sexual Abuse*, Oates, K., Tong, E., and McDowell, M. Department of Paediatrics and Child Health, University of Sydney and the Royal Alexandra Hospital for Children, Camperdown.

and clutch at anything which tries to bring some sort of understanding.

We do not know how many abusers may commit a solitary offence – it is so unlikely to come to light. We have many cases where the same victim is repeatedly abused, and many where there is more than one victim. Sexual abuse by strangers seems to be likely to be a matter of multiple victims, and the paedophile is a risk to all children.

The stranger who preys upon children is a menace from whom they need protection. Unfortunately when he is caught and sentenced, there is little, if any, chance of his getting treatment, however much he may seek it himself, and there is the constant and unjustifiable risk that he will be catapulted back into society and every likelihood that he will offend again. The child molester is a pariah, probably needing protective isolation when in prison, denied hostel accommodation when discharged, and often left to fend for himself in a lonely bed-sit, wander round the streets and parks and watch the children . . .

There is much more abuse within the home than outside it, and while some mothers and other female relatives may be the perpetrators, the preponderance is far and away greater among the males, possibly with tacit or explicit female collusion. Fathers, grandfathers, uncles, stepfathers and their relations, even older siblings, may abuse their relationship with children in a family; baby-sitters are not exempt, and as we have seen there may be more than one adult involved, and more than one child. The ultimate evil is the 'sex rings' in which a number of children may be involved by their parents in multiple sexual activities with a group of furtive adults; a number of such rings have been exposed by police investigators in this country, as well as abroad.

The characteristics to be found in offenders are obviously the focus of much research. Our difficulties in an area of very imperfect knowledge are similar to those in other areas covered by this book: there is a wealth of non-specific factors and a dearth of real knowledge; again we have to beware of the insistent pressure for instant answers from professionals, press and politicians.

Personality features of the sexual abuser can be listed as including immaturity, poor self-esteem, confusion of role as an adult or parent, difficulty with relationships with other adults, lack of inhibitions and plausibility. Denial of allegations is common (not unnaturally) but often this is meant as a denial that what was done was wrong, rather than that it had not happened.

While there may be deviant sexual appetites, and offenders are often those who have themselves been abused earlier in their lives, sexual assaults are often thought to be less sexual than attempts at domination, at abusing power. A man who finds adult relations difficult may seek to compensate by imposing himself on children, and feel that he can dominate in relationships with them at least, even though he is unable to with adults.

Not a lot is known about how best to treat offenders, although the obvious goal must be to get perpetrators to come to terms with their responsibility for what has happened to their victims, and to be able to live their lives so as no longer to threaten the safety of children. Cure cannot begin unless there is an acceptance of guilt and an acknowledgment of responsibility. Work must focus on restoring the family concerned by changing the nature of the relationships within it, perhaps by removing the offender or enabling his return under suitable safeguards. If, say, a father is deeply repentant and trying to atone, and the child needs his presence and is unlikely to make progress without it, how far does one let society's need to inflict custodial punishment override the needs of the child to recover within a reorganised but complete family? In the case of Philip Jones, for instance, restructuring the family relationships was the key to helping this four-year-old boy who had been sexually assaulted by his father. The child lived with his mother and father, great-aunt and two much older cousins in Hampshire. The incident came to light when a family friend learned that Philip had been in the garage with his father and had fled crying bitterly, saying 'Don't touch me.' Mr Jones was interviewed by the police and admitted under questioning that he had sexually assaulted his child. He appeared in court but was not finally convicted of an offence because it was felt that he was unfit to plead, having a mental age of only eleven years, although he had convictions of a sexual nature.

The family was extremely close-knit and it was difficult to get them to accept the possibility that an incident had occurred and to understand that the priority was the protection of the little boy. No one wanted to believe that anything had happened in the home. It became apparent that the great-aunt was acting very much as Philip's mother, and his natural mother, Mrs Jones, had very little say in his upbringing, although she was trying to break away from the home environment. A council house was quickly found for Philip and his mother.

While help was provided for the father in a regular day-care facility centre, Philip and his mother came to know each other very much better and developed a good relationship. Mrs Jones had been influenced by her extended family and felt that her husband had not been responsible for doing anything to her son. However, she gained a great deal of independence; she became more assertive, and able to care for her son and to tell her extended family what was best for Philip. Initially there was concern because of Philip's low weight, his regression in toileting and his unwillingness to attend a local nursery on his own. Gradually, however, he started to gain weight and settle into the playgroup. Now he makes friends easily and is a happy and well-cared-for child.

In other cases criminal procedures may be necessary *per se*, and also appropriate in establishing responsibility and its acceptance, but how they are followed through needs to be established after careful evaluation of this tension between the needs of the child and the sanctions of society. Some offenders may seek help and ask for treatment that will enable them to stop; prison may still be the likely outcome, and it has to be faced that remorse, however strong and sincere, does not necessarily mean that there will be no recurrence. We must err towards being safe; and we need to be able to do so without making the aftermath of the abuse an even greater ordeal for the children.

Characteristics to notice in children suffering from sexual

abuse are similarly general, but any child who seems disturbed in any of the ways listed below should have proper attention, and the possibility of sexual abuse should be borne in mind as one explanation. Behaviour to look out for includes:

Aggressive behaviour, or severe tantrums.

'Don't care' attitude or detachment.

Excessively compliant behaviour.

Undue watchfulness.

Sexually explicit behaviour inappropriate for age-group.

Sexual aggressiveness and open masturbation.

Child only happy when at school, and yet often kept at home.

A 'loner' with few friends and little participation.

Distrust of adults, noticeably of close family.

'Tummy pains' with no medical justification.

Eating problems – too much or too little.

Disturbed sleep, nightmares, bedwetting.

Running away from home.

Suicide attempts/self-wounding.

Some of this behaviour could of course relate to any one of a number of disturbances affecting a child, and the first reaction of someone concerned with a child must be to ask, 'Is there something wrong which needs professional attention?' Somebody sympathetic and trusted by the child should try to establish if there are any worries, and, most importantly, believe what the child is saying, in the first instance. If you have borne sexual abuse in mind, and the child's story, or behaviour, make that seem a viable suspicion, seek professional help – from the NSPCC, social services, general practitioner, health visitor, or the police.

The immediate objective must be to secure the care and protection of the child, and this applies both during investigation, and in the longer term. Decisions have to be taken about how best to help the family, and about how to deal with the offender. There may be those who question why any thought should be given to perpetrators; the strongest reason is the effect upon the victim, who needs to be protected from it happening again, to be freed from guilt, and to be helped to get over the experience.

The best place for protecting the child will usually be within the family, but this will not always be so. Removing the suspected perpetrator from the home may not be enough – if, for instance, there was more than one, or if the mother is incapable of protecting. It is important to consider whether the child is safe, if there are other children and whether they are safe.

Victims need to be reassured (if their claim is true) that they are not damaged. They need to be convinced that it is not their fault, even if they said 'yes'. Medical examination will be essential, to establish facts, obtain evidence, to check for injuries needing attention, to exclude sexually transmitted disease, which now must include AIDS, to check on possible pregnancy, to reassure, and to dispel fantasies and worries based upon ignorance and fear. Other evidence will need to be sought – soiled clothing, bedding, pornographic material.

The environment for examination, and the attitudes and techniques, obviously need great sensitivity and experience, and doctors, particularly paediatricians and police surgeons, need to work together, preferably to a pre-arranged procedure. It is helpful if there is a designated centre, such as a specific hospital paediatric unit, which is a focus for special facilities and skills, and the NSPCC has begun to develop examination facilities which are more homely than a police station can manage to be, to form an unthreatening 'neutral' venue for medical examination and for disclosure interviews, using video-recording techniques when these are agreed.

Those who do this work need to understand children, be able to relate to them sympathetically but without senti- mentality, and to understand children's language, verbal or non-verbal. Use of dolls, puppets, play or drawing materials can all help a child to express themselves, and anatomically correct dolls are becoming increasingly sophisticated in the range of adults and age groups they represent.

Sexual abuse is an offence, and when it is discovered the police must be involved; this is a legal requirement, and the increasing sensitivity and skill of police involvement is leading to joint investigations with social workers, which are more effective, and also mean fewer disturbances for the child. Interviewing must be focused upon the child, and considerations of the rules of evidence must determine the approach. Sensitive supportive questioning is needed to gain the cooperation of the victim, and if well done it can have a marked therapeutic value in itself.

As I have said, video-recording at this stage can help to reduce the need for repeat interviews by other interested workers, and I hope that it will not be long before suitably conducted interviews can be taped and used as legal evidence. Parliament has already agreed that live video can be used to make testifying less traumatic for abused children; to date it has not accepted video-recording. This attitude shows an acceptance of a principle but a denial of its most effective implementation.

In the United States it is claimed that, after seeing a video-tape of their child's evidence, up to 80 per cent of abusers will plead guilty, which can spare victims much ordeal. Proper use of the technique can also benefit the case of the innocent defendant, whilst making it less easy for the guilty one to go scot free in the many cases in which the facts are there but they are not in legally admissible form.

Treatment of the child should focus on the child, but should take the family as a whole into consideration. In some cases rehabilitation of the offender may retard the child's recovery; in others, where there is sufficient acceptance of responsibility by the offender, willingness to change and evidence of change, his returning to the family may enable a new start to be made and proper relationships to evolve.

A most important step forward today is the degree of recognition that we have a problem, and the Cleveland débâcle must not be allowed to affect that. I believe that the bringing of this deeply repressed child-torment out into the open is probably the greatest single contribution yet made to prevention. It is now more difficult for evil or foolish men to think that they can get away with dark and sinful deeds. The one-time comfortable reassurance that 'even if she does try and tell, no one will believe it of *me*' is being replaced by the worrying realisation that perhaps they will. The cogent injunction, 'This is our special secret, girlie, that only you and I know about,' can now be countered by, 'But it is a bad secret, not a good secret, and I don't have to keep it.' Any illusions which a perpetrator may have had before that his actions were not bad for the child have been shown up for what they always were – a defensive rationalisation.

However, there is still an enormous amount to learn. We are dealing with critical and intimate areas of feeling and relationships, and need always to be aware that 'putting things right' can look very different to the traumatised child, unless we try to look at what we are trying to do through the eyes of that child. There is no room for complacency, and anyone who claims to know all the answers is greatly to be feared. We need to have still greater public awareness, to strive to increase our understanding, to devote more resources to research and to make great strides with professional training.

Chapter Seven: Emotional Abuse

The emotional, or psychological, abuse of children can take many forms, some of them obvious, others quite surprising and even, to any thinking parent, rather disturbing when we look back upon our own behaviour in bringing up our children.

For emotional abuse to be proven sufficiently for a case to be placed upon the Child Abuse Register, it has to be satisfactorily established that a child's behaviour or emotional development have been severely affected, and that assessments by doctors and by social workers have found evidence of either persistent or severe neglect, or rejection – and a sense of rejection is what scars so deeply. The mechanism for deciding whether or not an allegation of emotional abuse has been substantiated – as in any other form of cruelty – is the 'case conference', a meeting convened in accordance with local child abuse procedures, when social workers, doctors and other professional workers who have knowledge of a family, pool their experience, examine the evidence and agree on appropriate action.

A woman in a north-east coastal town telephoned the NSPCC because she was very upset at having hit her twelve-year-old daughter Sarah. A visit was arranged and the tearful mother confessed that her attack on Sarah had followed one of their frequent bitter arguments, and that the girl now had two black eyes to show for it. The mother had a long history of severe anxiety attacks needing hospital treatment, and because of her continual ill health when Sarah was a baby the little girl had been looked after for long periods by an aunt and uncle. It became apparent that bonding had never taken place between mother and daughter. The mother had never been able to love or hug or caress Sarah; she didn't even feel able to touch her. In further interviews it was apparent that she hated her daughter and she came to admit that she didn't want her in her home at all. Her boyfriend said that he was constantly frightened that Sarah would be hurt and repeatedly tried to intervene during their arguments; the trouble was that he was not always around when they happened.

For her part Sarah was obviously emotionally a very damaged girl: she was extremely withdrawn, backward in her behaviour and had difficulty in communicating her thoughts and feelings. She was very pleased to think that she might leave home, but had no clear ideas about what she wanted for her future. At first she was taken into voluntary care, but after a case conference and a full assessment by a psychologist, arrangements were made for her to be placed with foster parents.

While this example demonstrates some of the factors in emotional abuse cases – and shows how one form of abuse so often merges with another – one can only begin to grasp the range of problems that can occur by first considering the needs of a child if it is to be able to develop physically, intellectually and emotionally. If one then looks at the factors that apply to a particular child, a pattern can be appreciated of the different ways in which children can suffer if these basic needs are not met – whether through neglect or deliberate act by the parents. Of course, many of the factors I shall mention can relate to other circumstances, and one can all too glibly pick upon a particular action by a child – like seeming to be withdrawn – and draw a false conclusion. There can be many reasons why a child is withdrawn upon a particular occasion – it may be bored, or have toothache. That is why I referred to behaviour or development being 'severely affected' and to the need for medical and social assessments to bear out the misgivings which have arisen from, say, persistently withdrawn and unusual behaviour. It is the whole picture that needs to be considered, not individual pieces.

When looking at whether a child is being deprived of some of its needs to an extent that is abuse, one needs to look at all the factors, and at the child. How old is she? Are her needs being met in a way that is consistent with her age, and general state of development? Does she have physical or mental characteristics, be they disabilities or extra strengths, which modify the position? Are there any factors of culture or class to take into account? It can be misleading to interpret a family position on the basis of a 'snapshot' – a brief glimpse of behaviour – without being able to find out if it is part of a general pattern, and if it reflects the dynamics of child/parent relationships.

The needs of a child can be considered as having five basic facets or 'ingredients'. If we look at what these are, and at different ways in which a child's needs may not be met, we can begin to understand some of the ramifications of emotional abuse and neglect.

1. Care and Protection

The need is for adequate physical care and protection, including medical attention when appropriate. This means making sure that a child is properly fed, appropriately clothed and protected from the elements and from outside dangers, washed, changed, given proper rest and exercise, and that within this general care there is the expectation that positive health care will be given and that medical help will be sought, and sought promptly, whenever necessary.

Children need to have a sense of security. This is so strong that even when parents are providing the most appalling homes and standards of care, removing a child to a 'better' home may do more harm than good, because what sense of security there is will be damaged and destroyed, particularly when a child is too young to understand. But there can of course be circumstances when that damage is judged to be a lesser evil than the risk of leaving a child where it is.

Factors that diminish a sense of security within the home can be very obvious when a disorganised household gives no continuity, for instance when the parental role is shared around between a number of people who go through the motions of feeding or clothing, but don't really care, give no consistency, give no love. There may well be a lack of physical needs being met, even episodes of physical abuse, but the main theme is one of disordered indifference.

This type of experience can be garnished in many ways. Parents may be preoccupied with their own problems of marital discord, violence or mental illness. Their example may be the very last 'model' of ideal conduct for any child to absorb if there is to be any hope for it to achieve a stable life for itself, maintain any sort of marital relationship when it is older, let alone achieve a secure and properly managed home for its children in their turn.

Sometimes there can be a 'Fagin effect'. Children can be exposed to criminal influences or experiences. In England today there are many Oliver Twists who have been exploited by older relatives to gain entry to houses or to take part in organised shoplifting. They can also experience activities that are quite inappropriate for their ages: while one hopes that the authorities will take steps to enforce the Video Recordings Act 1984, one of the reasons for it receiving such strong support when it was before Parliament was evidence of children being allowed – or even made to sit up late at night to watch video films showing appalling violence or corrupt sexual practices. What a way to be introduced to 'the facts of life'!

While failure to thrive, or grow, can usually be ascribed to physical problems (whether of disease or of lack of proper care) there are undoubtedly cases where the stunted growth of a child is due to lack of loving care. Not long ago the NSPCC had such a case: a boy, from a prosperous home, who was so deprived of love, so emotionally neglected, that his growth was retarded. He was 'an emotional dwarf'. When he was removed from so unsatisfactory a home to loving foster parents he rapidly shot up to his proper height.

Such physical signs of emotional neglect are understood and accepted as valid, but they are rare. The scars of being rejected and unloved are not often so outwardly visible, although let no one doubt how real and painful they can be. More often they are hidden, and the cause of so much pain that they are well guarded from enquiring eyes, however caring. They can show through changes in behaviour which give a clue to something being wrong; what that may be can sometimes be quite clear, but more often much patient searching, done with trepidation that one may be adding to rather than relieving a child's difficulties, may yield a range of possibilities which need to be explored before a judgment can be made.

One emotional casualty is the clinging, irritatingly submissive, insecure child who will go to almost any lengths to be noticed, praised, wanted; sadly this very attention-seeking behaviour can have the reverse effect and cause rejection from those the child most wants to be responsive. Even to be slapped for being an irritating nuisance can mean the satisfaction, of course, of at least getting some sort of attention. Another is the sadly worldly-wise youngster with a pseudo-maturity of behaviour.

One such child was eight-year-old Judy, who was the eldest of six children (the youngest three being from her mother's re-marriage) who lived in a small town in Northern Ireland. This was a wretched case, taxing, time-consuming and often soul-destroying for those who tried to reach out to the children. There was a whole range of social problems in the family, including suspected non-accidental injury, financial crises, emotional conflicts and a poor marriage. The case came to the notice of the NSPCC from the local Social Services Department when a doctor confirmed that facial bruises on Judy's six-year-old brother were non-accidental.

Various forms of practical help were arranged to try and help this family – family aides, day nursery places, home help provision – and over an eighteen-month period the NSPCC made over a hundred home visits, despite threats of violence to the worker concerned.

Throughout this period the main concern was for Judy. She was given responsibilities in the home that were fit only for an adult – for a parent indeed – to carry out, and which were quite beyond her physically and mentally. Her behaviour varied dramatically. Sometimes she was a 'good' girl – if unduly quiet. She would do household chores, take responsibility for her younger brothers and sisters, run errands. At other times she was a terror. Her behaviour at school was so

bad that she was expelled. She was guilty of repeated shoplifting and other criminal behaviour. When arrangements
were made for her to go to a special education unit her
attendance was very poor; her mother's help in ensuring
attendance could not be relied upon for she was too useful as
a household drudge.

This state of affairs could not continue. There was a lengthy
session at the juvenile court before the Care Order[1] which the
NSPCC had applied for was granted, on grounds of emotional
abuse. All but one of the children ended up in care. Some long
time later an NSPCC officer was approached by a smart well-
mannered girl who said, 'Remember me? I'm Judy!' Judy had
respected those who cared.

2. Affection and Encouragement

The need is for affection, approval and encouragement. To
deprive a child of affection is to subject it to cruelty. Love is the
very basis for a child's development of its own security and for its
relationships with others, and every child looks to those it loves
to show their approval when it tries to learn to move, speak,
think or act for itself.

Sarah, whose story starts this chapter, lacked love and was
withdrawn in her behaviour; she was given no encouragement or loving reward when she learned to do things – and so
she was a very backward child.

How easy it can be to put down a child seeking praise for
achievements which by adult standards may not be so special!
How hard it is to realise that from a child's perspective they
are an achievement indeed, and that the child desperately
needs the encouragement of a few kind words!

There are children who find that their whole life is one of
being denigrated by those from whom they most want to hear
just a little praise; sometimes it is by deliberately cruel mental
torture; more often it is in the form of indifference or total
lack of understanding of what it means to a child to be
noticed, to be wanted, to be appreciated. Often of course this
all reflects something that has been going on in generations of

[1] A Fit Person Order in Northern Ireland.

the same family, and the emotional flatness of one generation is being passed on to the next.

Sharon, who lived in a northern city, had three daughters aged from nine to three years old. Her home was almost painfully clean and tidy; the girls were well fed and well dressed. One day their father had suddenly walked out on them, and had not seen or heard from since – something Sharon just could not come to terms with, nor share in any way with her children.

Joanne, the middle child, had been very close to her dad and seemed to be missing him particularly. She developed a lot of behaviour problems, especially as she never heard from her father even on her birthday or at Christmas. She was naturally a lively child, and when she began to be 'difficult' her mother found her very hard to cope with – indeed the NSPCC became involved because Sharon had been seen by neighbours to be screaming abuse at Joanne and hitting her.

Being both father and mother to her girls was a great strain for Sharon, as any single parent knows, and what probably made it worse was that she did not feel able to talk to her daughters about their father. She needed to be able to give voice to her own hurt and anger at being deserted and to be able to confide in someone about her concerns over bringing up the children – yet another case of the relief that can come from the realisation that there are other people with similar problems. She had become so wrapped up in her own very real troubles that she had ignored the fact that her girls also needed to be helped with theirs, rather than have her becoming exasperated with them.

Contact with a self-help group could have been invaluable, but this was not available, apparently. With counselling instead Sharon came to realise that both she and her daughters would have to come to terms with the fact that father was not coming back to them; that they would have to adjust to managing without him; and that the girls needed to be able to talk about their changed circumstances. Helped by some funds to go on a holiday together, something they could no longer otherwise afford, Sharon began to feel that she could begin to cope again. There were friends and relations who could help, and while she had, understandably, been through a very bad patch, she now felt that she and her children had a future and could work towards it.

This acceptance and change in attitude affected the whole family for the better. Joanne began to relate better to her sisters, and while she was still quite a handful, she responded to Sharon taking a more positive role, and finding time to play with her and make her feel that she mattered. They did not face an easy future, but things were beginning to look up.

3. Stimulation

The need is for stimulation and instruction. An encouragement I have mentioned is the looked-for reward for achieving another step in learning. For an older child the promise of a reward may be the right stimulus; a younger one may need other ways of attracting its attention, such as a colourful toy to reach out for, to help it learn how to move its limbs and coordinate its movements. A baby will not learn to crawl if everything it wants is brought to it; it cannot learn to walk unless it is taught how to achieve its balance – after many false starts. Much of this learning is achieved through play, where loving encouragement and support not only help the child to acquire new skills, but provide the basis for emotional security. Some parents do not know how to play.

I once had a surgery in Brixton, where I can remember a family coming to see me one day, full of concern that their new baby was making no progress, and could not speak a single word. They were a large family, very wrapped up in themselves, and baby seemed extremely fit and alert. It certainly could not speak, and it did not take me long to find out why not: it didn't need to. That poor infant had only to grunt or whimper and the entire family was on the floor at once, all trying to work out what it wanted and supply it; there was not the slightest stimulus to say a single word.

A little while ago a conference of head teachers was told that there were children starting school these days who were barely able to speak, and certainly who could not begin to read or write. No one ever read a story to them, or encouraged them to learn any of the basic social skills. Poor children! What sort of chance do they stand in a competitive world if they have been given no opportunity or encouragement to learn how to speak and write and use words; to develop their imaginations; to reach the attainments of normal children in becoming potty trained, learning to dress themselves and manage simple tasks?

When first I joined the NSPCC as its new Director I visited a family centre where I was amazed and distressed to see young mothers being taught how to play with their own children. How deprived their own childhood must have been! It was a very poignant experience to see the growing joy with which they realised that there could be fun in life and that their babies were reacting so happily to the first play they had ever known. Indeed, when the children were put down for a rest, the mothers rather shyly picked up the toys and carried on playing amongst themselves. A whole cycle of deprivation was being broken as these young women learned to relax and enjoy their babies – and the babies loved it.

4. Discipline

A child needs proper discipline and control. 'Proper' means not too little – and not too much. I have already noted the distressing 'spare the rod and spoil the child' attitude across all classes and societies, when even royal princes would be beaten black and blue to make them obedient. The other extreme can also be bad; children need to have rules and boundaries until in time they can learn to set their own, and indeed for their own safety they must learn to obey some rules when they are too young to be able to understand why. If there is to be discipline there must be sanctions – punishments – and the form these may take has varied greatly in different cultures and at different times. The abuse of punishment can produce its own cruelty, of course, and while there is a strong movement against physical punishment today, alternative methods can also be used evilly in ways that can destroy a child's self-confidence.

The word 'discipline' has tended to become linked with regimented strictness and harsh punishments, but there are other meanings. One in my dictionary is 'obedience and orderliness'; another is 'self-control'. Children need to have some order and control in their lives; indeed, most of us want the security of a reasonably ordered life, although we may vary quite a bit in how far we depart from it. For a child especially, lack of an ordered pattern can be very disquieting, and the absence of any organisation in the home can mean that children will feel lost and insecure, and will lack the stimulus to achieve any self-discipline or self-control, to the extent, in some cases, of being uncontrollable.

Mary was the youngest of three children in a family from a town in the south-east which had gone to pieces after the father became seriously disabled in an accident; he lost his job and there were growing financial difficulties. All the children were wild and destructive when they came to the attention of the NSPCC, Mary in particular showing delayed development for a girl approaching four years old. There were suspicions that the children were being physically abused too.

Their home was filthy, cluttered and disordered, and everything about it was haphazard. Meals came when mother got round to it, and other aspects of child care she seldom got round to at all. Arrangements were made for Mary to attend a playgroup, and to make sure that she got there transport was laid on too.

When she first arrived at the playgroup, Mary could hardly speak a single word. She seemed to have a number of minor injuries, she was very dirty indeed and her feet were encrusted with dirt; she was frail, withdrawn and had very little motivation to do anything. She was not potty trained and still wore nappies.

Her parents were very hostile and suspicious, and resented having the feeling that they were being watched. However, they began to respond to an honest approach from the Inspector, who made no bones about things that he saw as being wrong for the children, but who also started to gain their trust by making it clear that he was not there to preach at them and by just getting on with giving practical help and support.

Mary soon began to make progress at the playgroup. At first she had screamed and stormed when being taken from her mother, but as she began to settle her behaviour started to change, and she began to respond to having a more ordered existence and some pattern to her life. She began to talk, and in a short while was beginning to string short sentences together. She became potty trained, and while she still had far to go she had much better coordination of her movements. She began to get on better with her brother and sister.

Mary's parents began to take a real interest in her progress, and her mother in particular was very excited that she could talk. Both of them began to respond to advice and encouragement about managing their home and bringing some discipline into their life, and their children's. The father began to pick up in morale, and despite his disability set about painting and decorating the bedrooms. Meals were better organised, and both parents achieved a remarkable improvement in the way that the home was run; they noticed the changes in Mary's behaviour, and began to tackle the destructive and uncontrolled behaviour of the other children. They took more interest in them, began to tidy up the home and put things away, and were able to help all their children to achieve better self-control and purposefulness. There was still plenty of room for further improvement, but with every success came more incentive, and more self-confidence.

In the area of discipline, as in so many, it is really a matter of balance. Absence of routine, of any rules, can lead to disorderly or even delinquent behaviour; if children are not taught self-control (and taught by example too) they can fail to learn how to tolerate frustration, or control their anger, which can be very destructive to their relationships and thus to their own futures. On the other hand children can be crushed by having too much rigid routine, can be cowed by too much discipline, and when they get older can rebel against it. Probably one of the more difficult balances for parents to strike is that of adjusting their standards as their children grow; the ordered routine and unquestioning obedience of the infant need to progress to a more flexible – but still stable – pattern for the teenager; he or she will still need some limits to be set, but in a way which allows self-confidence to develop and the 'self' to grow – because each child is increasingly a person with a right to individuality, and must not be treated as an extension of either parent.

5. Appropriate Independence

Children need to be helped to grow into independence. This can be one of the most difficult needs to meet. Adults themselves may want to keep their children's dependence on them in order to feel secure and wanted, and it is not always easy to disentangle the parents' wants from the children's needs. Sometimes the most crushing rejection of a child can come in the truly emotional abuse of destroying – or trying to destroy – his or her capacity to advance opinions, develop preferences, achieve friendships or make up his or her own mind about something.

The last of my 'ingredients' is the right of a child to be helped to a degree of independence appropriate to his age. Some children may need to be held back from being more aggressively independent than they have the experience to manage; others need to be encouraged; above all parents need to be able to separate out their own ambitions for their children from their children's needs to be able to have ambitions of their own.

'If you don't apply for medical school your father will be deeply, deeply disappointed; he's always wanted you to become a doctor!'

'But Mum, I don't want to study medicine! I want to be a journalist!'

'Oh! How could you be so selfish, John? After all your father has done for you!'

I wonder how many readers will recognise some similar incident in their own family? It can happen in reverse too. I remember counselling a young man who wanted to become a mature entrant into medical school, because his father wouldn't let him apply for medicine as a school-leaver: 'Ambulance driver is good enough for you, lad! I'll have none of these airs and graces about doctors – just you keep to your station in life!'

As children grow towards adulthood the last thing that they need is unfair pressure to do the things their parents want that are part of the *parents'* ambitions; adolescence can be a hard enough period to grow through without added stresses like that. Excessive rigidity by parents, leaving no decisions to the child, is bound to lead to low competence in doing things independently, to lack of confidence and to an unhealthy over-dependence which may be flattering to the parent but which is cruel to the child. Children need to find activities of their own, and friends of their own, and while parents should lay down overall guidelines (where will you be, when will you be home, or other relevant limits) for the children's safety, they should be encouraging their offspring to explore to the extent of such limits and to have a growing feeling of autonomy, of trust and of responsibility.

All parents may recognise some of these faults in their upbringing of their own children; to make mistakes is only human. But to hamper excessively a child's development may cause a failure to thrive, a restriction of intellectual growth, a destruction of a child's individual personality that constitutes an abuse of the child which may well have effects into adulthood.

I think that it follows from this exploration of some of the facets of emotional abuse that there is a very complicated and varied range of hurts and deprivations, many of which are unconsciously inflicted, and which can range from the trivial to the deliberate and sustained intent to crush a developing person's personality and self-confidence.

Some degree of unintended slight is probably unavoidable, and children need in their own interests to learn to cope with being teased, snubbed or unfairly treated – and not to be too sensitive to the knocks of everyday life. We cannot create a totally ideal world, we cannot indeed always expect a fair one, but we can try to recognise that every child is a distinct person and needs to be respected as such. There is still a great tendency to regard children as chattels of their parents, to be treated as the parents wish, when the 'rights of parents' exist only in so far as they discharge their duties to their offspring.

Most people would agree that callous and overbearing mental bullying is unacceptable, and could accept that on occasion it may be necessary to split up a family rather than have a child virtually destroyed. Such cases are not always recognised, proving them may be difficult and lifelong casualties may result. What is more common is the almost unconscious cruelty of ignoring a child's needs, or ambitions, in order to promote one's own satisfaction. The scars of emotional abuse may not be outwardly visible, but they may nonetheless have longer lasting consequences than physical injuries.

Chapter Eight: **Why Do Things Go Wrong?**

In 1987 there were two major inquiries into child abuse deaths. One was that of Tyra Henry in the London borough of Lambeth who suffered severe bruising and bites and died as a result of a fractured skull caused by her father, Andrew Neil; the other was that of Kimberley Carlile, in Greenwich, London, who died at the hands of her stepfather, Nigel Hall, and whose injuries included multiple bruising, dehydration and malnourishment. In addition, and overlapping them, was a judicial inquiry which the government set up under Mrs Justice Butler-Sloss after a furore in Cleveland over what seemed to be the simultaneous mass removal of a large number of children from their homes and families because of alleged sexual abuse; there was great controversy over the diagnostic methods, and perhaps even more about the process of protection being apparently so radical and disruptive.

It is ironic that almost in successive weeks there was widespread condemnation of the social workers in Greenwich, claiming that they were inadequate for failing to remove a child from an abusing home (almost to the extent of branding them as accomplices to murder), followed by equally hostile criticism of social workers in Cleveland for being so cruel as to remove children from homes which consultant paediatricians had declared to be unsafe.

Indeed, the most disquieting element of the media response to child abuse tragedies is that there is sometimes what appears to be almost a malign focus on social workers as a profession as well as on the individuals involved, from which other professionals are spared to an illogical degree. In the

Jasmine Beckford case, for example (she died in Kensal Rise, London, aged four and a half, as a result of injuries inflicted by her father, Morris Beckford), the inquiry report in 1985 – *A Child In Trust* – recorded grave errors on the part of magistrates, and medical and health professionals. These were ignored by the news media, who fixed their attention upon the social workers involved and seemed intent on hounding them out of their jobs – and any other jobs they might subsequently succeed in getting. Likewise with the Kimberley Carlile tragedy: the inquiry rightly recorded professional errors on the part of the social worker mainly involved – which he himself with great integrity had already admitted – and drew attention to failures on the part of other professionals, including a health visitor and a doctor; but although the media severely criticised the social worker, the other professions received no media attention, presumably because the understanding that any of us can be capable of human error on occasion is acceptable except in the case of social workers.

The inquiry report about Kimberley Carlile, *A Child in Mind*, referred to the fact that there have been thirty-five inquiries into child abuse deaths since the case of seven-year-old Maria Colwell, whose tragic death in Brighton, caused by her stepfather Mr Kepple, had led to great public outcry, and thus triggered off the start of child abuse procedures such as the NSPCC had been advocating. The cry has therefore been taken up: if there has been this number of avoidable deaths since the Colwell Inquiry in 1974, what is going wrong? Is there any point in the present child abuse procedures? Is all this money and time and effort being wasted?

What I would prefer to see is a more responsible approach of putting admitted and tragic professional failures into a balanced perspective. Assuredly, there have been errors and they should not have been made. All of us, however skilled and however caring, who have to make value judgments about the behaviour, and probable future actions, of our fellow human beings are bound to make errors of judgment from time to time. This is not something to be proud about, or to dismiss without taking what steps one can to minimise error, but it is an unmistakable fact. Human beings are fallible and can misjudge situations; this applies not only to social workers, but to all of us – even judges, doctors, teachers, policemen, priests – and parents.

Of course there must be concern when something goes wrong – but surely the seriousness should be assessed partly on the individual case – for every death that is preventable is that much more a tragic one – and partly on how it compares with the generality of cases? In order to judge whether the fact that since 1974 there have been thirty-five cases where public opinion (or media demand) has been so stirred that a major inquiry has resulted represents a good or bad record, we need to take account of how many cases there have been that have *not* resulted in inquiry.

I would estimate that in the same period there would have been, at the least, 2,000 child abuse deaths where the risks the child faced were not known to any professional worker; and that there would have been somewhere between 100,000 and 200,000 established cases of physical abuse alone, which were under care of the social services in their areas, or sometimes of the NSPCC, which have not resulted in the need for inquiries, and where for the most part there will have been a satisfactory outcome.

When giving evidence to the Cleveland inquiry, the President of the Association of Directors of Social Services referred to the fact that there were some 30,000 children on child abuse registers at that time. If in two or three of all those cases there is professional error, or even professional negligence, does that mean that the whole system is a failure? Thirty-five inquiries since the Maria Colwell case works out at two or three a year.

At the end of 1987 a significant report was published of the Confidential Inquiry into Perioperative Deaths – deaths, a proportion of which were deemed to have been avoidable, occurring during or after surgery. The death rate was of the order of 7 deaths per 1,000 operations, of which more than 1 per 1,000 were 'avoidable', the rest the surgeons and anaesthetists probably could not have prevented. The reasons for the avoidable deaths varied – wrong decisions being taken by doctors too junior and inexperienced to have the responsibility, for example.

There was no outcry about these figures. The public recognises that life and death decisions, particularly at moments of emergency when the right people are not always available, will not always turn out for the best, although those concerned will have been doing their best. This is a proper, understandable and civilised approach.

But compare the attitude of the news media to social workers. In 1987 there was at least 1 avoidable death per 1,000 surgical operations – no comment. In the same year there was at least 1 avoidable death per 10,000 (or more) physically abused children – outrage! Are social workers expected to be at least ten times cleverer than doctors? I hope that I may be forgiven, as a one-time doctor now responsible for supporting the activities of over 400 specialist social workers, for sensing a degree of hypocrisy in the difference in attitudes to these two professions.

Nonetheless, there are deaths and lesser mishaps in child abuse case management that could be avoided. It matters little whether they are 1 in 1,000 or 1 in 10,000; any is too many. We need to ask what goes wrong, and how can such deaths be avoided?

To try to answer these questions, we need to consider two very different matters. The first is this: after a gruesome child death, the question 'how can we make sure that such a thing never ever happens again?' is a vain and foolish one. We can never hope to eliminate all greed, jealousy, rage, lust or violence. We can do our best to reduce their harmful outcomes on defenceless children, and one way is by trying to identify children most at risk and by defining how best to protect them. We can try to remove the ignorance and misunderstanding which lie at the heart of so much of the misery which adults cause to their young. We cannot eliminate all such harm, be it from the uncontrollable sudden rage, or from the coldly calculated and sometimes subtle violence of the wilful offender. And if a child dies, it is not the social worker who has killed that child; it is the person who did the deed. Perhaps there were those nearer to the family than the social worker who could also have done something to prevent a fatal outcome.

The second matter is to look at the various professional involvements, whether of individuals or of 'agencies', who have a role to play in the upbringing and the care of children, and to see what can be done to improve the effectiveness of the protection they can, or should, provide. There are various ways in which this can be tackled; I have approached it in the same way as the government appraisal of child cruelty inquiries (see *Child Abuse – A Study of Inquiry Reports 1973–81*, HMSO, 1982).

The main legal provisions relating to the response to children who are being or might be abused come from the Children and Young Persons Acts of 1933 and 1969. Local authorities (acting through their Social Services Departments) have statutory responsibilities across the whole of their communities. These include their duties to offer care and protection to children, to investigate allegations of abuse or neglect of children, and to take steps to ensure their safety.

By contrast, whereas social services are *required* to act, the NSPCC is *empowered* to do so; its officers are 'authorised persons' for whom there is legal provision to take care proceedings for the protection of children and to prosecute parents for cruelty. In practice there is little difference, for the Society's own rules place obligations upon its social work staff, its 'Inspectors', to use their time-honoured title – or the 'Cruelty Men' to use a phrase just as long established – which amount to an acceptance of as much duty to respond as applies in law to the local authority.

The third agency with statutory powers is of course the police, whose frequent involvement in child abuse cases can be initiated in a variety of ways. The family or neighbours may approach the police first if there are fears about a child's safety or whereabouts; they may be called in by professional workers if there is evidence of violence, or difficulty in gaining access; or they may be called if social work investigation reveals possible criminal behaviour, such as sexual abuse of a child.

The police, the social services and the NSPCC, are the three agencies recognised by the current government guidelines as having a justified right, despite the need for inter-professional collaboration, to take legal action independently and even, if they feel it necessary, contrary to the majority view of a case conference. This is not intended as a provocative move, but as an essential one in the interests of child safety. If an experienced police officer, or child abuse social worker with the NSPCC or the local authority, is uneasy about a group decision, and has a hunch that a child is in more danger than has been agreed, then he or she should not allow the group's attitude to deflect from professional or statutory duty.

There has been controversy about police involvement in child abuse procedures, some of it political. In recent years there has been a considerable shift of emphasis in the role of the police in child abuse matters, and the way that these three 'statutory agencies' interact in child abuse matters provides a very useful study in the development of professional collaboration in this field.

The earlier inquiries, such as that into the death of Maria Colwell, drew attention not to the lack of professional skill on the part of the police, but to the fact that they had tended to keep their information to themselves and not share it with social or health service workers; this in fact demonstrated just one of the means by which children fall through the protective net. So many of the child abuse deaths that could be classified as 'avoidable' have happened because knowledge that could or might have saved them, and which certainly should have led to better informed professional protective action, was not available to the right people at the right time. The professionals who possessed that knowledge or information did not share it in a way that would have made it available across the professional community.

Neither the police nor any other professional group should be singled out as having any particular failing in this respect; inquiry reports have also shown that hospital casualty departments, specialists, general practitioners, health visitors, NSPCC officers, social services personnel, school staff, nursery workers and others have all had different pieces of information which separately may have been inadequate to justify taking action to protect a child, but which taken together could have provided strong grounds for concluding that a child was at risk and that urgent action was necessary.

An important ingredient in the lack of sharing of information has been a lack of understanding (or downright misunderstanding) of each other's roles, responsibilities, professionalism and purposes. Some reports have also shown that this lack of awareness has meant that others, with relevant knowledge of events threatening to a child's well-being, have not been consulted as they should have been. One inquiry found that the matron of a nursery school had information about a child that could have been crucial in saving its life; however nobody had thought of consulting her, or even of letting her know that there was concern about the family. Had she been consulted she would have realised the significance of her experience.

School teachers can play a vital role, and very many do. But this role has been less than adequately provided for in their training, or in their being consulted; it is not unusual for a teacher to be worried about a particular child in her class, only to be told when she shares that worry with a superior that there is no need to do anything. There can be few people better placed to notice changed behaviour in a child of school age than the teaching staff.

The police and the NSPCC have had experience of working together for over a century. So close was the relationship in late Victorian times that the commissioners of both the City of London and the Metropolitan forces instructed their officers to pass all child cruelty or neglect cases on to NSPCC Inspectors, who in those days also wore uniform and were often looked upon as 'children's policemen'. Nevertheless there have been occasions when collaboration has not been all that it could be, and there are bound to be such instances in any relationships.

In the last two decades the development and growth of departments of social services within the local government framework has outstripped all previous municipal provision, including the statutory responsibility for child protection; they now provide far and away the largest input into this field

of activity, as just one part of their whole range of responsibilities for responding to social needs throughout their
respective communities. This period of rapid growth, complicated by major reorganisation of local government, and in
the full glare of often very hostile publicity, has added to the
burdens of an emergent profession establishing itself in the
public confidence and achieving its own professional ethos.
The recommendation in the Seebohm report that social
workers should be 'generic' – have a common or generalist
professional basis – may have been right as a long-term
measure to improve cohesion in a new profession that was an
amalgam of various previous roles; but in the short term its
rigorous interpretation meant the sudden loss of specific and
valued skills such as those of the Children's Officer, and the
Psychiatric Social Worker.

After a period of what seemed to be almost uncontrolled
growth, expenditure upon social services was placed under
tighter control. At first this could be seen to have a beneficial
effect: the value of different activities came to be better
assessed; support in the community, rather than residential
care, was realised to be a cheaper, and generally a better and
more humane option in the case of many family and individual problems. Unfortunately the pruning of expenditure has
continued and essential services are being eroded. Some
London boroughs no longer have enough social workers to
deal with the cases of children already on their child abuse
registers; this means that even where cruelty or neglect have
been established as happening, there is no professional
worker who can supervise the family and make sure of the
safety of the children involved – let alone can allegations of
what could always be life-threatening abuse be investigated as
promptly as is necessary.

The NSPCC policy for its staff is that any alleged incident of
child abuse should be investigated urgently, within a maximum
of twelve hours. *A Child in Mind* suggests that the time limit for
social services and all workers should be twenty-four hours.
But if there are no social workers available, what can be
done? When things go wrong, and a case is mishandled, as
sooner or later is bound to happen in the best regulated

department, a proper concern that professional negligence can be eliminated, and that the nature of the erroneous conduct should be discovered, must take into account the resources that were available. These resources may be time, skills, people or finance.

Conscientious workers can be confronted by an unacceptable dilemma: faced with an impossible workload, too few colleagues and inadequate support or training, do you work at the pace which you can responsibly manage, ignoring all other cases because you know you cannot cope with them, whatever possible risks are being faced by the children involved? Or do you cut corners, race around as many cases as you can, taking snap decisions which you hope will be right – but aware all the time that you could in your haste be missing vital evidence and taking the wrong decisions? What do you say – more significantly, what do you *feel* – when the apparently safer family problem which you ignored in favour of one which worried you much more turns out to have been anything but safe? How do you cope with always knowing that you are having to take chances? These are impossible dilemmas.

The NSPCC has also undergone significant changes, but while it has come close to a 1,000 per cent increase in its income over the past ten years, it cannot possibly manage to fill the gap. A decade ago its Inspectors, no longer in uniform, were diminishing in number and in some areas losing credibility because they were too few and too scattered to provide a coherent service; and this service was too vaguely defined. It was only in those places where there was a sufficient concentration that the traditional child protection service could be maintained, despite the commitment of individual officers.

At the same time, and following a sabbatical period spent with the Society by Dr Henry Kempe, a new pioneering development began of Special Units, which were teams of child abuse workers, established and usually funded jointly with Social Services Departments. Beginning in Manchester, and spreading to a dozen other cities and counties, these teams worked to a clear remit of managing the child abuse processes, including management of the register and case conference procedures, providing treatment to a limited caseload of selected serious abuse families, and offering training and consultancy services to others.

Taking advantage of its centenary in 1984 the NSPCC was able to restore its finances, and restructure and expand its services, now based upon a network of seventy child protection teams. These teams, each comprising at least six qualified social workers as well as other staff, are modelled upon the special unit concept in that they function as teams, have a specific defined remit achieved in consultation with the local authority and other professional interests in each locality, but maintain the 'Inspector' tradition of twenty-four-hour availability to the general public, offering counselling and advice, and ensuring such further response as may be necessary by whichever of the three statutory agencies may be most appropriate. Training and consultancy are also offered to local professional groups and courses.

The function of the police has been evolving too, with more emphasis upon their supportive involvement within the community, as well as the primary task of providing a law enforcement agency. Some of the family involvement that was the particular task of women police tended to disappear when they were amalgamated with the main force and ceased to have a separate role, but this has been restored with men and women officers being involved in community and juvenile work. It is noteworthy that the police do not only have a role in child abuse work when their particular law enforcement duties are involved, or their access to records or past offences may be needed. They have their own pro-fessional skills and experience to add to the multi-professional approach: for example, a police officer at a case conference about alleged abuse may have no specific information to contribute, but can greatly help colleagues in other disciplines to assess the information that they have before them and identify both what further evidence they may need before reaching a decision and how to obtain it.

Within the Health Service there is a whole range of professions, and over the years there has been evidence from

8. *Perfectly adequate facilities reduced to squalor —
the picture cannot convey the smell*

*9 and 10. These two
photographs were
commissioned to illustrate
the work of the NSPCC.*
Models are used to ensure the
anonymity of those families
with whom the NSPCC works

11. *Absolute despair reflected in the demeanour of this abused and unloved child*

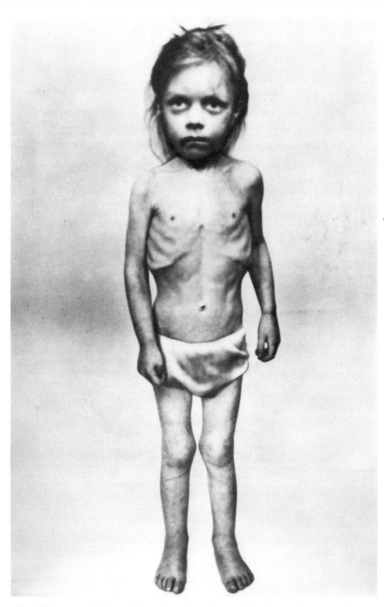

12. With a stepfather who refused to acknowledge her existence and a mother too frightened to help her, this four-year-old child was being slowly and deliberately starved. She reached the point where she was feeding herself out of dustbins. It didn't happen in the famine stricken third world, it happened in a British town (like the one you live in)
To protect the child's identity the face has been changed

time to time of lack of communication between them. I have already mentioned the reference in some inquiry reports to hospital departments, often the Accident and Emergency Dept, (Casualty), being part of a communication gap also involving general practitioners and health visitors. Again, the basis for this failure has so often been a lack of understanding of each other's role, pointing to deficiencies during training; professional workers need not only to learn their own skills, but to be aware of how their work relates to that of others if they are all to give of their best to the public they all exist to serve.

When I was a medical student nearly forty years ago 'non-accidental injury' and 'the battered baby syndrome' were unknown terms, describing unrecognised concepts. Nowadays the General Medical Council formally states that doctors have a duty to report cases of child abuse which overrides their duties of confidentiality.

Doctors, whether in hospital or in general practice, have an important role in practically all cases of child abuse. First, they may be best placed to raise suspicions from their various types of contact with children, whether for routine checks or for more particular reasons of ill-health or injury. Second, their professional knowledge is so very often needed when abuse is suspected by others and a medical opinion is required to confirm or contribute to the diagnosis. Third, they may be needed to give evidence for the courts when there is a question as to the safety and custody of children.

It is sad to have to relate that the recent attention paid by Mr Louis Blom-Cooper QC in the Kimberley Carlile inquiry to the importance of regular medical assessment of children, and to the charting of growth and height on percentile charts, can be traced right back to the Maria Colwell report. This had stressed the importance of medical assessment as a baseline for monitoring children's progress, and of identifying un-acceptable departures from normal development so that they could have appropriate attention. If Maria had had regular medical examinations, as the report pointed out, and vital data had been routinely recorded, attention might have been drawn to the steady deterioration in this poor child's condition – and her life might have been saved.

Fifteen years later, much the same could have been said about Kimberley Carlile. She was taken to the doctor on one occasion, about retarded speech, but although he was specially experienced in child health he does not appear, from the record reproduced in the report (*A Child in Mind* p. 45), to have carried out any routine examination. When she died the following summer, Kimberley, by then aged four and a half, weighed just over 2lb more than when she was a two-year-old. An opportunity might well have been missed for demonstrating severe failure to thrive before her life was in danger, which could have reinforced the need to take action.

The government study of inquiry reports in 1981 showed that social workers were involved in every case; and in all the inquiries but one there was a health visitor involved, and in all but one a general practitioner. These two professions have a very particular role.

The health visitor has a duty to monitor the welfare of all young children and is notified of all new births so that he or she can visit the children in their homes, to help and advise about their care and upbringing. Liaison with general practitioners can help to identify families with young children who have moved into the area and who otherwise might not be known about.

Their role is that of *health* visiting, and is not primarily a child abuse one; but regular surveillance of families, and monitoring the attendance of children for immunisation and for health checks, provides a unique vantage point for overseeing the adequacy of the home and of parental care and interest. Are the children happy, and developing as they should? Or are there matters for concern – failure to thrive, signs of neglect, or suspicious injuries? Does one child always seem to be missing, and if so, why? A vigilant health visitor will always be asking such questions.

The health visitor's task begins where that of the midwife finishes. Midwives may see very little of the subsequent development of children they have brought into the world, but they have a very special relationship which develops during ante-natal care, and which reaches its climax during confinement, to assess the mothers and to note those who seem poorly equipped to cope with motherhood; it is their role both to try to help them and to pass on the information for the family doctor and health visitor to pick up. If a young mother shows antipathy towards her new-born baby that is a danger signal that should not be ignored.

The GP, as the family doctor, does not make routine visits in the same way, but he should be in a position to know the whole family, and over a series of contacts to have a general overview which is unmatchable when the family is stable in one place and stays with the one practice. The doctor should be able to see each child regularly for preventive medicine checks and procedures during its early months of life, as well as when there are episodes of illness or injury in the family. Each child has its own NHS record which should follow from doctor to doctor throughout its life; the record envelope should contain routine information about development, immunisations and other landmarks, as well as notes about consultations for any illness. All reports from hospitals and clinics should be there, and many doctors have special markings to alert themselves and their colleagues to special features needing attention in the notes, such as difficulties at the time of birth, unexplained injuries, or any other worry about the child, or indeed the family.

Positive findings should be there too, for it is just as important to be able to dismiss false alarms. If a baby seems puny and underweight, a note in the medical record that gives a natural reason for this can save unnecessary worry for all concerned. The family doctor's records, and personal knowledge of patients, can be of crucial importance when child abuse is suspected. They can produce evidence that will refute unfounded suspicion – or that will reinforce the misgivings that have arisen from other signs and so alert workers to invoke child abuse procedures and protect the child from further risk. It follows that if the records are inadequate, or are not consulted – or are not produced – it can be that much more difficult to reach the right decision about whether there is a need to protect a child.

Some of the most disadvantaged families can of course be those that slip most easily through any protective net. They have 'no fixed abode' – and if they are on a doctor's list it may well be one who is many moves back in another town. The health visitor may have no knowledge of their existence within her area, their medical records may be fragmented and widely dispersed; some members of the family may become known to social services, but especially if they bear different names the true size of the family – even the existence of younger children – may be quite unknown. Members of the family, or neighbours, may be the only way any problems come to light.

However, inquiry records show that there have been cases where things have gone wrong, and where crucial information has been available – but has not been communicated. The GP has not known of the health visitor's worrying findings, or the health visitor has been ignorant of previous episodes that have been recorded by the GP.

If one looks at the hospital services one can find comparable problems – hospital maternity unit staff who can observe and should communicate early warning signs; nursing and medical staff in accident departments who note unusual circumstances, but may not communicate the '?Child Abuse?' entries in their records to those health and social workers in the community who need to know.

The Children's (or Paediatric) Department of the hospital has a particularly important role. Indeed it is quite common for hospitals to try to avoid the communication problem, and to ensure that all suspected child abuse and neglect is dealt with expertly and consistently, by designating a particular paediatrician, or paediatric unit, as the referral point for all such cases, so that there is one focus for information, and a specialist team for all investigations. This system can work well, but can be burdened by its own success; a formidable workload can develop, and 'designated' paediatricians can be so deluged with child abuse cases as to be unable to attend to their many other clinical duties to sometimes very ill children.

Still, things go wrong. Nobody ensured that Maria Colwell was registered with a family doctor, and there was no power to *require* medical examination. (If she had been registered with a doctor, once there was such a formal doctor/patient relationship he could have ignored any parental view and insisted upon examining her.)

In 1975 the Auckland Inquiry (following the death in Sheffield of Susan Auckland, aged one year four months, following gross physical abuse by her father) noted that the hospital doctor, family doctor, community doctor and health visitor all knew that the child was being discharged from hospital to a home where there had already been one child killing – but no one alerted the social services. Six years later the Mehmedagi Inquiry following the death in London of Maria Mehmedagi, aged eleven months, from gross physical abuse by her father, again stressed the importance of proper information being communicated by a hospital when discharging a child back into the community. In some such cases there were other failures of communication: the neighbour knew, but left it to the social workers to find out for themselves – why?

Lack of communication can have other reasons. In Liverpool, when anxious relatives felt that the social services were not protecting Darryn Clarke (who died in Liverpool aged four years one month following gross physical abuse by his mother's boyfriend, Charles Courtney), they reported to the NSPCC. The Inspector involved, hearing of the complexity of the case, decided that it would be unprofessional to bring any further interference into a family that had problems enough and already had social services involvement. He therefore took no action, which was directly contrary to NSPCC procedures. There might be those who would defend his decision, for assuredly there must be many disadvantaged families where an excess of professional interferers has tended to do more harm than good. However, had the Inspector even communicated with the social services, he would have found out that they had lost track of Darryn's whereabouts. His death soon afterwards might have been averted if the new concern voiced by relations had been passed on and responded to – as it should.

Much comment has also been made in various inquiries about the state of law and the adequacy or otherwise of knowledge of the law on the part of professional workers. The Carlile case is but the most recent of many where key workers were found to be ignorant of the law and of their legal authority to act in gaining access to a child about whose well-being there was concern, or to insist upon a medical examination. What seems to have had less attention is the balance between three factors – the adequacy of the law, the adequacy of knowledge of the law and the adequacy of the use of professional authority.

In 1981 the DHSS concluded that 'Child Care Legislation is extensive and complex'. That remains true today. The government has carried out an extensive review of child care law since then, and has acknowledged the need for a single comprehensive new Act of Parliament. All are agreed that it is urgently necessary, but Parliamentary time does not seem to be forthcoming.

The latest comment about changing the law was made in *A Child in Mind* which triggered off a Private Member's Bill in an attempt to meet one area of need – that of obligatory medical examination – although this really should be something that is provided for in an overall enactment.

That same report also showed, however, that several social workers who had been involved in Kimberley Carlile's case had been ignorant of what legal procedures had been available to them and were undecided how to act. The procedure that was available to them – that of convening a case conference, which would have revealed the extent of the professional worry, was not resorted to. With hindsight it is so easy to ask why not. It hardly matters what the law may provide for, or what child abuse procedures there may be, if key personnel are ignorant of the powers and processes that are available to them.

Likewise there must be the will to take the action necessary to safeguard a child. This means that there must be the security of confidence in one's duty to that child, of capacity to form a coherent plan of action, of experience in coping with the conflicting pressures, *and of confidence in being supported and supervised*, by a manager who knows the score, and who has the experience, skills and knowledge of the law and child abuse procedures that are essential to good management.

If the will and the self-confidence are there, other provisos may matter less. Shortly after the Second World War an ex-serviceman decided to emigrate to Australia, which was not unusual, and to sail there himself, which was. His 'ship' was a war surplus landing craft of dubious seaworthiness, but no worse than his seamanship. What caused concern was that he proposed to take his family with him, including a baby. He would not accept that this was an unacceptable risk, despite public outcry.

The NSPCC therefore instructed its Inspector at Dover, the port of departure, to stop the boat from sailing. How to do so was left to him. Undeterred by what the law provided, or even if it did, he put the regulations to one side and acted. The family returned from their last trip ashore to find that their boat was no longer afloat in the harbour – it was well and truly grounded, high up on the harbour wall, and hemmed in by baulks of timber and chunks of concrete. The Inspector had used a bit of resourcefulness and explained the problem to the dockers. The father accepted that, however valid his purpose, the means were inappropriate and called off the venture. The process that persuaded him was anything but orthodox, and should not be used as a precedent today, but in that particular case it ensured the safety of the children.

Analysis of what went wrong in particular cases is important, but it can never provide the whole of the answer for it can only provide a part of the story, and it must not be taken too far. Most inquiries into avoidable child abuse deaths have – rightly – focused upon one case where things went wrong, in one area, involving one group of workers in one particular set of circumstances under one variety of child abuse procedures. Was the error, or succession of errors, typical of those people, of that authority, of those procedures? Even if it were, would any conclusions to be drawn necessarily apply across the country? And what about the cases that went right?

I believe that there is something to be learned from every case, but also that there can be danger in drawing too general a conclusion from particular circumstances. We must avoid being too specific, and look to draw general conclusions in a general way. If we can draw back from the particular we can achieve a clearer view, and can draw several broad conclusions as to why things go wrong in some child abuse cases.

First, we cannot prevent all child deaths – some happen in such secrecy that we do not even know how many there are. Even when suspicious circumstances come to light, there will always be the possibility of errors of human judgment, which we must do our utmost to guard against, but can never entirely eliminate.

Second, there must be sufficient *resources*. If there are not enough social workers to deal with *known* cases of abuse in an area, let alone to have time to investigate *suspected* cases; if they do not have proper support, or opportunities to keep up to date with their training, or facilities for sharing information, let alone have enough time to deal with each case – then it does not matter how caring, competent, or committed the individual, risks will unavoidably have to be taken, and mistakes will unquestionably be made; no one can foresee which errors will be fatal, nor which corners can be cut without tragic consequences.

Selection of those who specialise in child cruelty work is obviously important, and the need to have such specialists available to professional workers in every area should not need stressing further. However, specialists cannot be consulted if those whose work brings them into touch with children – doctors, nurses, teachers, social workers, playschool leaders or the public – fail to spot possible danger signals and respond to them. The training of all professionals – or the lack of it – has so often been an underlying problem revealed in successive inquiry reports: lack of training as to the law and how to apply it: lack of confidence in one's own role, and of understanding of the roles of others; lack of awareness of the significance of observations which should alert concern; lack of experience of the dangers of identifying with parents or other adults to the extent of wanting to believe explanations which do not fit the facts; lack of training in the vital importance of heeding the children.

It is no good if people are isolated in their own professional attitudes, if they do not know what to look out for, nor how to respond when they do find problems, or worrying suspicions.

All professionals working with children need training about child abuse in their basic curriculum, and this foundation needs to be built upon throughout their careers by regular up-dating on the job – and in the company of other professionals they work with. Only thus will mutual understanding, respect, cooperation, and *communication* really happen.

Time and again the key workers in mismanaged cases have lacked the supervision, management and support that they needed. Child abuse work is difficult, demanding, emotionally stressful and often physically dangerous. Those engaged upon it need to have managers who understand all this, and can provide proper support; who need to have their own training in managing and supervisory skills, as well as competence in child abuse matters. They need to be able to help their staff avoid becoming so emotionally involved in cases as to lose their perspective, and to spot if a worker is identifying with one of the adults in the family in a way that can be manipulated. They need to supervise each case, and be sure that investigation has been adequate, consultation and com-munication have taken place, that there is a clear plan of action, and that the children and the parents know what is happening. Sadly, in case after case one finds that such support and guidance have been lacking, and that often inexperienced workers have had to fend for themselves, or indeed have even had their concerns about the urgency of a case played down.

Most of all, things have gone wrong when there has been failure to listen – listen to neighbours, teachers, playgroup helpers, 'non-professionals' – particularly to *listen to children*. It is so much easier, especially when you do not want to believe that children are being wronged, to accept an adult's story as a satisfying explanation, and to fail to look at the children, note their attitudes and behaviour, and listen to what they are trying to say. 'Listen' may not always be quite the right word; 'heed' may be better, because with young children especially it is not what is said but how it is said; and it may not be in words but in behaviour, reactions to what is said or done, or the story may be told by drawing, acting and playing out situations using toys or dolls.

The question that needs always to be asked is 'How can we reduce the incidence of such tragedies?' The answer lies in better training, better resources, better support and supervision, better cooperation and communication and in a better informed and more understanding public, with every adult ready to speak up when children appear to be suffering. Above all, the answer lies in listening to the children themselves.

One unfortunate development has been the Government's rejection of carefully prepared proposals by CCETSW (Central Council for Education and Training of Social Workers) to increase the basic training course in social work from two to three years. If child abuse is to be tackled more effectively, social workers need the opportunity of better training.

More regrettably, I am not yet in a position to comment on the Cleveland Inquiry Report. I can only express the hope that its effect will be to prevent a reaction against the greater public awareness of child sexual abuse and growing professional competence in responding to the children. The idiosyncratic behaviour of one group of professionals in one area at one particular time must not be allowed to appear as the norm. The number of cases allegedly discovered was *not* unreasonable; the hiatus in procedures was to be regretted, and I hope that there will be guidelines on the necessity for multi-professional input into diagnosis, and on the necessity for setting patterns of remedial action which will cause least disruption of home life to the children – that will minimise further trauma to *them*.

Chapter Nine: **What We Can Do**

Child abuse is a topic that is talked about far more nowadays, which in itself is very important for children. In the first instance, if people are more aware that children can be abused and neglected, they are far more likely to be alert to suspecting abuse when they see signs of it – signs that otherwise they would have missed, or put aside as being unthinkable. Children are more likely to be rescued, or helped, if adults are on the alert.

The need for this awareness and alertness applies to everybody. Parents, relations, friends, neighbours, teachers, playgroup workers, health visitors, nurses, doctors, social workers – everyone who comes into contact with children and cares for their well-being.

Awareness can help these people too in another way. Parents in particular, but also everybody with the regular or occasional charge of children, can be alert to asking themselves, 'Am I handling this the right way?' This can apply to so many things. Is a child having the right care and protection? Is it getting the right stimulus to learn to move, to learn to think, to speak, to grow self-reliant, to develop a sense of values – good/bad, right/wrong?

Finding the right balance between giving a child room to develop in his or her own way, and leaving him or her without enough discipline, learning how to strike a mean between being over-protective and under-protective, are constant challenges of parenthood. Without an awareness of how things can go wrong for children, the very existence of such a balance, and of the need to strive for it, may not be realised by parents who blithely do what seems right to them, possibly because that is how they were brought up themselves, but without having thought whether the way that they treat their children is really the right way and in the interests of those children.

There are still those who, whilst rightly proclaiming that children need discipline in their lives, and a code of conduct (which is what discipline really means), can be over-fierce in how they enforce it, and not realise the harm that they do, when they mean to do good. As we have seen, a child can suffer from too much discipline, but equally from a lack of it. Some years ago I met a patient of mine in the street, pushing her little boy in a wheelchair. All his milk teeth were rotten – he just had a row of black stumps along his gums.

'This is too many iced lollies, isn't it?' I mentioned, pointing to his teeth.

'I know, doc,' she replied, 'but he does insist upon having them!' The boy was not in a position to judge the effects of his liking for ices; his mother was, and her constant giving in did him no kindness.

An awareness of the need to see things from the point of view of the child, and of the child's interests – even though that view may be in conflict with the long-standing tradition that parents know best and can do as they like – is important.

There is another benefit from greater public awareness of the possibilities of child abuse, in that it allows light into dark areas that were previously unsuspected or ignored. We have seen that sexual abuse has been allowed to flourish for so many years because people did not know, or want to believe, that it was so prevalent, and so tended to reject any evidence that was presented. If someone did, very tentatively, mention to a parent some worry as to what his daughter had been saying, they would be all too ready to accept any assurance on his part that this was a mischievous assertion by a highly imaginative little girl, who would be spanked for her trouble! The greater likelihood was that the little girl's story would have been roundly rejected in the first place.

But as I have discussed in Chapter 6, in the light of current knowledge children are building up confidence that they will be believed and responded to, because adults have a better awareness. Also, molesters must be increasingly aware of this awareness, which will clip their wings. The parent or relative who seeks sexual gratification from a child with the injunction 'This will be our special secret! Don't you dare tell anyone!' will now know that children are being taught that there are 'good secrets' which should be kept, and 'bad secrets' which shouldn't – and will know too that other adults will be more ready to believe any stories the child might tell. Likewise, the baby-sitter who plays inappropriate games in the bath, or when undressing a child, will be less tempted. The light of knowledge provides an umbrella of protection for children.

This umbrella is there too when parents or others choose someone to take care of their children, or to be in charge of children's activities in the community. The knowledge of the risks of abuse can make people alert to the need to check on the record of anyone offering themselves for such jobs; and people who offer themselves, and who care about children, should understand and respect – indeed they should support – the need for credentials to be checked.

There are special areas where being alert to the potential for child abuse is particularly important. As we have seen, doctors seeing injuries should always consider how the injury happened, and whether the story fits. If a child needs special treatment that means removing a baby from mother, the doctor needs to bear in mind and provide for the fact that separation could threaten bonding. Nurses and midwives can be the first to spot potential difficulties from the behaviour of a young mother at the very time of birth, or indeed of a mother-to-be, and preventive measures can be set up. Likewise, all other professionals, such as teachers, social workers and anyone who is in contact with children, should be alert.

It is natural that a common reaction whenever a disturbing case of child abuse becomes news, or there is media comment about the latest statistics, is to say 'What can we do?' The first answer to this basic question, therefore, is to say 'Be aware', and being able to put the news in proportion is part of that awareness. If some tragic death of a neglected child is labelled as 'the worst case in living memory', apply a pinch of salt and reflect that for some sensationalists 'living memory' means, roughly, 'since last week'. If some professional worker is branded as a criminal accomplice to the death, rather than accept the judgment without question it is more helpful to try to take a balanced view, and as reasonable people we should try to have an idea of the strains and stresses that are involved in making right judgments; there may have been negligence, or inefficiency, but it is more constructive to view them in perspective.

When a major (and costly) inquiry is demanded 'to ensure that a tragedy like this will never happen again' it is important that people should be aware that inquiry reports have been published about twice a year since the death of Maria Colwell stirred the public interest. None of them has stopped anything happening again. A single inquiry can cost hundreds of thousands of pounds, providing lucrative employment for a large squad of solicitors and barristers to represent all and sundry, and to protect their respective clients' interests at great length, when, if that money were to be devoted to staffing, training, and management support of professional social workers and others, there would be a better chance of fewer errors being made.

A Community Concern

While child abuse is indeed a family problem, and can reflect a variety of malfunctions within a family, the fact that it takes place is a matter of concern to the whole community, and the problem will only start to be properly tackled when the whole community takes an interest. I have already suggested areas of concern to various sections of the community and mentioned their need to be aware of the problems, alert to spot them and to be self-examining in their own behaviour; that awareness may need to be followed up by informed action.

One of the most important preventive actions that can be taken by people within a community is to act with a community spirit. Are there facilities in the community where children can be cared for, can play and enjoy recreation appropriate to their needs, which can help them to grow and develop, and give their parents a break too? Can the local community set up a playgroup on a voluntary basis? Are there facilities for single parents to have some support? Has any experienced person the scope to form a group on self-help lines, so that parents who are under stress, who feel a bit helpless and inadequate in starting to bring up a family, can find that there are others in just the same position, or who, having been in such a position and begun to gain self-confidence, can support and help each other?

One of the dangers of talking about the need for a 'community spirit' is that the term can seem to be impersonal: individuals within the community can all feel that it is someone else's responsibility – it is easy to say 'Why don't "they" do something about it?' when 'they' means 'anybody as long as it isn't me'. Another way of putting it is to speak of neighbourliness; the community spirit is our duty to have respect for our neighbour and to have concern for our neighbour when something goes wrong. When the milk stays uncollected outside an old lady's door, it is neighbourly to pop round and see if she is all right, or needs help. When an old-age pensioner spends long hours visiting his sick wife in hospital, it is neighbourly to provide a little casserole or other prepared food for him. It is part of the philosophy of 'love thy neighbour', still practised in some communities.

It is of course easier for any of us to love the neighbour we like already, or identify with as 'one of us' – but that description does not always apply to people living near by who may need our help that little bit more, and who might often be children. Indeed I had been talking about this when addressing a meeting, and afterwards a lady told me that my remarks had reminded her of an incident in her own rather lovely village. A man unknown to them had been imprisoned for some criminal offence, and his wife and large family moved into a house in the village. Word soon got round about their background and they found themselves shunned by most of the community. 'We don't want that criminal family mixing with our kids' was the general reaction.

Then, as Christmas approached, and plans were being made for the Christmas party for all the village children, someone mentioned this pariah family. It was Christmas, and they were lonely and unhappy-looking children, who looked as though they could do with a decent meal. This came as a rather uncomfortable suggestion at first, but shamefacedly everybody agreed that it was more than time for them to do something for a family that was fatherless for no fault of their own. It was decided to invite them, and one of the villagers went round to call on the family and offer them this belated welcome. She was very distressed to find how deprived this poor family was, and how glad the mother was that something was being offered to the children.

It was quickly decided to try to do rather more, and in particular to make it a community responsibility to give some support to the family – a sort of collective substitute fathering. Furniture and clothing were found, and the mother was befriended and given a chance to feel that she belonged somewhere, and that there were neighbours prepared to help her to cope. Christmas presents were provided for all the children – otherwise they would have had none. They were nice children, who soon made friends, and people felt a mixture of guilt that they had ever thought or acted otherwise, and of pleasure that they were now having such a happy impact; they were very touched a little later when a letter came from the distant prison, saying how much the father appreciated his family being accepted into the community in a way that had made so much difference to their lives – and to his. He hoped to be able to express his thanks in person before too long. On his discharge this did indeed take place, and he too came to be accepted into a community which had become that much more of a community because of this episode.

There are many, many occasions when a distraught young mother, trying to cope with advanced pregnancy, a brood of dirty, poorly managed children, and in danger of sinking beneath her burdens, desperately needs a caring neighbour who can help her, but if she looks forlorn, and the children ill-kempt and dirty, the likelihood is that we will all spurn her. Like the prisoner's family, she needs some actual help in getting on top of managing how to feed, clothe and care for her children; she also needs the human contact of someone who cares, that bit of neighbourliness that can give sufficient uplift of spirit for her to regain the will to keep going.

When I went, one snowy day, to inspect a house which had recently been vacated by an NSPCC Inspector who had retired, I found a pile of parcels and shopping bags outside the door, protected by a large bush, and took them inside, when I could open the front door against the pile of mail and circulars that had come through the letterbox. The bags all contained Christmas parcels, intended for children. What touched me most about this thoughtfulness to offer loving gifts to unknown children who had family problems was that some of them had been labelled 'For a girl aged 7–9', 'For a boy about 12'. What touching extra care, for strangers the givers would never know! Among the envelopes which had come through the door were a number of greetings for children being helped by the NSPCC and money to buy things for them, including one new £20 note. It was not a wealthy neighbourhood, nor a particularly law-abiding one, but the ex-Inspector, when I wrote to him, told me that this custom had been maintained for well over twenty years to his knowledge, and nothing had ever been stolen from under that bush.

The Test of Caring

I have described some simple but marvellously effective acts of neighbourly love, which may be direct, or anonymous, and which enrich both the giver and recipient, and which help to sustain community life. Their impact upon families which are at the edge of despair can be electric. The force that comes from personal involvement should never be underestimated, and for many who face difficulties in their homes and their private lives the caring act of a loving neighbour can do more than the skilled intervention of professional workers, or can enhance and enrich what the professional contributes.

There is one specific involvement for neighbours, when it comes to dealing with child abuse, that can take great heartsearching and worry to undertake, and yet which can be literally vital – life-saving – for children. That is to take the responsibility for reporting to someone in authority a suspicion

– that a child or children is being abused; has been seen with bruises; or is seen seldom out of doors, and only rarely as a wraith at a bedroom window.

'Are you asking us to be snoopers?' is often the retort to this suggestion. There is a very proper concern not to be a Nosey Parker neighbour, and in some communities there is a very strong tradition of mutual self-protection from all outside intervention. As a GP in Brixton, called to an emergency in a house I did not know, I would often be met with bland indifference as to whether the family I asked about lived there, until it was realised that I was not a policeman, or other official, but 'the quack'.

There can be several facets to this anxiety about being a prying neighbour. There is the understandable attitude I have already mentioned; but it must be realised that this can partly be based on the old tradition that what parents do to their own children is entirely their own business – when it isn't. An indifference to being involved can also be comfortably explained away as not wanting to interfere. More seriously there may too be a fear of being identified as the sneaking neighbour, which can be embarrassing at best, and physically dangerous at worst.

Another difficulty that needs to be overcome is that of identifying with the child's position, when for any adult it is so much easier to relate to that of another adult. An example of this attitude appeared in the *British Medical Journal*, when an unidentified doctor complained that family doctors should not be expected to report suspected child abuse cases, as by doing so they would be breaking faith with their patients. What he failed to point out was that a battered baby is a patient too.

For that is the crux of the matter. No one wants to encourage prying neighbours; the snooper has never been a popular person in our way of life, even if he was performing a public duty. But adults have a duty of care towards the helpless, and if there are signs, or even worrying suspicions, that a helpless child is at risk, *who else is there to act for that child?* A baby cannot get on the telephone and say, 'Help me! I am being starved (or beaten)'; it is up to the neighbour, the relative, the health visitor or the doctor to report a suspicion and initiate the child abuse procedures. They may not always be justified suspicions, but that is better said when a professional has checked on the facts.

It is in fact very often the case that what look like very suspicious circumstances may have a different appearance when properly investigated; in which case there is all the more reason if worried about a child's well-being to inform a professional agency which can find out the true position.

The neighbours of a service family once notified the NSPCC that they were worried that they had seen nothing of the young baby next door. The husband was about to be posted to an overseas unit. What had happened to baby?

An Inspector called to find a young mother at home on her own. Yes, she had a small baby, but as they were about to go abroad and had so much packing and preparation to do, baby had gone up to her sister in Scotland to be looked after for the moment.

This was a plausible explanation, but the Inspector's manager was not satisfied, and enquiries were made through our sister organisation, the Royal Scottish Society for the Prevention of Cruelty to Children. They soon reported that there was no such address as the mother had given for her Scottish sister.

So the Inspector went back to the house. 'Come on, love! Where is this baby of yours?' The young woman burst into tears, went to a cupboard under the stairs and produced a brown paper parcel that contained her baby's dead body. The young couple had been terrified when they found their baby dead in its cot. Would they be charged with its murder? Would her husband lose his service career? Their grief and their fear that a cot death might be interpreted as being due to criminal behaviour (with perhaps an understandable but unjustified doubt as to whether they had in some way been neglectful for their baby to have died so suddenly) meant that they took the course of action best designed to bring suspicion upon themselves.

Fortunately in this case all was satisfactorily settled, but it might not have been, and the Team Leader's proper decision to check up on the mother's story of her child's whereabouts might have led to serious consequences when the tale was found to be false and the concealed death had been discovered. What is particularly apparent is that the neighbours had been very right to voice their concerns – there had been a criminally concealed death, which could well have been a criminally caused one.

Some child deaths have, sadly, happened when professionals have failed to take proper account of a neighbour's calls; but in other inquiries the evidence has been all too clear – neighbours come forward afterwards to say that they knew all along and 'the social workers should have found out too' – but they were never told what the neighbours knew.

The importance of people outside the immediate family needing to be ready to act as informants so as to protect children was borne out by the Judicial Committee of the House of Lords – the highest Court of Appeal in this country. The NSPCC had been taken to court by parents who demanded the right to know who had informed against them. In the Court of Appeal (Lord Denning dissenting) it had been held to be necessary to the cause of justice that accused persons should always have the right to know who their accusers were and to be able to challenge them. However in the House of Lords this decision was overturned.[1] Their Lordships endorsed the principle of a citizen having the right to know, but they made the important exception that this could not apply in the case of referrals of suspected child abuse; otherwise cases would not be noticed, could not be investigated, and children would continue to suffer and to die. Their Lordships held that the principle of protecting helpless children was more important than that of identifying informants.

This was a great relief to the NSPCC, which had felt the issue to be so important that it had taken the extremely

---

[1] Law Report, 2 February 1977: *D (Married Woman)* v. *NSPCC*, Before Lord Diplock, Lord Hailsham of St Marylebone, Lord Simon of Glaisdale, Lord Kilbrandon, Lord Edmund-Davies.
    The National Society for the Prevention of Cruelty to Children is entitled in legal proceedings to refuse to disclose the identity of a person who brings to it a complaint of a child being neglected or ill treated under promise of confidentiality.

expensive step of fighting the case all the way. The Society had jealously guarded the confidentiality of anyone who reported suspected cases, and does so to this day. Any person worried about a child must be reassured that they will not be identified; the lives of children are too important to risk losing any information that might save them.

Likewise when a case has been opened, the record maintained will be treated confidentially. Informants will not be told the details of what has been found, for this is private information. It will need to be shared, of course, within the necessary community of professionals, so that experience can be shared, information can be checked and the best possible (or least bad) decisions can be taken. But even within this 'privileged' professional sharing, the identity of informants is not disclosed.

Self-referrals

As will have been apparent from some of the cases quoted already in this book, there are many instances when parents, far from trying to conceal their maltreatment of their children, know what they are doing is wrong, are worried about it and long to be helped.

Sometimes this will be by direct contact: 'Please help! We can't control our son, things are going wrong, we don't know what to do!' There can be many variants on this theme of a direct plea for help, but common to them is an admission of a problem, a concern that the child is or will be suffering in consequence and a wish to get something done about it. Often there will have been advice from a relation or a neighbour, as when a young mother came to see an elderly Inspector and said, 'I'm having problems with my nipper – Mum told me to come to you, for you're the man who helped her when I was a nipper and she had problems with me!'

'What we can do', when 'we' are the parents involved, is certainly to seek out help before a bad situation gets any worse. One natural anxiety mentioned by parents in this position is shown by their trying to bargain: 'I won't tell you unless you promise that you won't take my children from me'

– a natural enough fear to express, and one that can lead a professional worker to make promises that could be wrong. If parents are worried enough about their management of their family to seek expert help, it is unlikely that they will need to be separated from the children in the interests of immediate protection of any child's life.

However, even if it does not seem likely at first sight, there may be reasons why such a promise could not be kept, in the interests of the children, and so it should not be made. A professional relationship with a family must be based upon integrity if it is to serve a useful purpose. Investigation may show that certain relationships within the family, or the degree of strain in the home, are such that a cooling off period is needed, and some temporary separation should be arranged while things are sorted out and a reunion can be worked towards. It is not unknown for a situation to be far worse than had been suggested, and for a child to be discovered to be at far greater risk from the other parent, or someone else within the home, than can be acceptable.

The answer, then, to such bargaining is to be supportive, but honest. 'I understand your worries: of course you don't want your children to be separated from you, and nor do I. But if I am to be of any help to you, you and I need to know where we stand with each other, and that will never happen if I make false promises just to get your confidence. You are going to have to be able to believe what I say. The last thing that I want to do is to break up a family – my whole job is to try to keep families together, by helping them to get things right. But I must always put the children first. You have already shown your concern for your children by coming to me for help, so surely you will know in your heart that if your children's safety really depended upon it, I might have to arrange for them to be looked after while we sort things out. If you care about your children you will have to trust me and then we can get on with helping you.'

The referral from parents may be less direct of course, and this applies especially when a caring parent is worried about the behaviour of an abusing one, but does not wish to be seen to have caused any trouble. The girl who asked the NSPCC to supply some cot blankets for her new baby (page 16) did not dare to say that her husband was beating their child; she hoped against hope that someone would not only supply the blankets but also look at the baby.

For many years the NSPCC found that about a third of all its cases were brought to it by the parents themselves, and it was very important that reassurance should be given that would help them to come forward and seek help. Analysis of different types of cases shows that the proportion varies; in cases of neglect comparatively few parents either realise, or if they do realise, will admit, that they have a problem. Now that the NSPCC is placing a greater emphasis on higher risk cases, the overall numbers of self-referrals is rather less.

The source of referrals to the NSPCC is illustrated in Fig. 3 (page 17), which also shows how many relatives face up to the question of 'What we can do' by bringing their worries to the NSPCC. If they have been unable to persuade a young couple to cope with a situation, or to seek help for themselves, they will show that their caring is genuine by reporting the case and achieving the help they know to be needed.

Local Procedures

Amongst the developments that were activated following the furore after the death of Maria Colwell was a government circular that advised local authorities to establish formal procedures for coordinating the reporting and management of child abuse in their various areas, which would include setting up registers and the establishment of 'Area Review Committees' which would have no formal authority, but which would act as coordinating bodies representing the local authority social services, the police, the NSPCC and all the health and welfare agencies concerned with children. Some of the effect of these procedures is discussed elsewhere, and the committees are being re-named, but what concerns us in this chapter is that many of them have produced not only procedures as to how child abuse cases are to be managed locally, but very helpful and informative booklets which tell people what to do. These provide guidelines on how to be alerted to possible child abuse and what signs to look for if you do suspect it; and a series of 'What do you do?' checklists, for different people in the community – teachers, play-school workers, doctors, detailing who to contact and what to do.

It can be well worthwhile finding out what information is available in your own area. A variety of local sources – the local authority, library, Citizens Advice Bureau, NSPCC – can guide you to the Area Review Committee, ARC, (or Joint Child Abuse Committee, JCAC, as it is beginning to be called) and the source of local advisory literature.

In summary, what we can all do is as follows:

1. *Be Aware.* Be alert to the existence of, and various forms of, child abuse and watch out for it.

2. *Try Prevention.* In your own family, try to keep well informed about the needs of children, and to understand how to meet those needs – and do not be afraid to ask for advice. Try to be a good neighbour, and reach out a helping hand to those who seem to be in difficulty.

3. *If you are worried that a child is at risk, put your duty to that child first and tell someone.* In an emergency go to the police. Otherwise contact the Social Services Department of your local authority, whose telephone number will be listed under the heading of the appropriate council; or contact the NSPCC, which maintains a nationwide telephone network twenty-four hours a day, and whose number should be listed in every directory under 'National Society for the Prevention of Cruelty to Children'. And do not rest until you have a response.

Try to avoid using anonymity. The NSPCC will listen but many people won't, and it makes it more difficult to investigate a case without being able to have better contact with the person worried enough to make a referral. How different authorities react to confidentiality I cannot say; the NSPCC will always respect it, and quote the House of Lords judgment on '*D vs. NSPCC*' (p. 154) to anyone who challenges it.

DO NOT HESITATE IF YOU FEAR THAT A CHILD IS IN DANGER. Do not wait until some terrible child tragedy makes you pluck up the courage to act – the tragedy that happens could be the one you were able to prevent.

Chapter Ten: **Protection**

The Dilemma

The first question that all of us ask when we hear tales of child cruelty is, naturally enough, 'What can be done to prevent it?' Prevention is of course the most important long-term aim. The problem is, however, that it is not the most urgent one. I often feel an affinity with the fire service: their first priority needs to be the prevention of fires ever happening, but how can firemen ignore a call to protect people already at risk when their house is on fire by saying, 'Sorry! Today is our day for giving fire prevention talks – we'll come another day'? So it is with child abuse: however much we want to strike at the causes, we cannot ignore the plight of children who are already suffering, and our most urgent need is to respond as quickly as possible to any cry for help and to protect children already at risk.

Ideally there would be enough time, that is enough money, to have people doing both, but while there are not enough people with the right skills to go round it has to be protection that is the most urgent call on the time of those who are available.

'Putting the Child First'

One of the most glib remarks that we can make is the one that the child must come first. We say it in our homes when seeing a television news report; we repeat it in professional circles; judges say it in court. All of us are then in danger of doing precisely the wrong thing for the child, because we've said something we think we really mean, and haven't thought about it – and certainly have not tried to put ourselves in the child's position. A child's perspective is different, as demonstrated by the story of the small girl who disliked church: when someone bothered to try to find out why, it was to learn that the child had no idea of what was going on, and that all she could see in serried ranks ahead of her was row upon row of amply proportioned rumps of the adults who towered above her tiny figure.

It is so much easier to say 'We're grown-ups and we know best' – and then to follow the adult line. It is much easier to achieve a relationship with the parents; we can take them at their word, and believe that what they say is best for the child. But it might not be. A parent may be covering up for his or her partner and manipulating the professional worker's reactions. Families that feel threatened can be very powerful in the way that they present a story that puts off the outsider. They can be threatening. They can be wheedling. They can be misleading about what is really happening and about what the child's position is. But 'putting the child first' means listening not just to the parents but also to the child. This may seldom be listening to a conversation as with an adult, but understanding what a child is expressing in behaviour, drawings or attitudes, and relating that to proper professional knowledge of the needs of a child of that age in those circumstances.

A little while ago there was a court hearing where a mother sought to have her child restored to her from foster care. She was a woman who had had two children from incestuous relationships; she had not been able to cope with either child, they were both in long-term care and she showed no love for them nor interest in them. She then had another baby by a new boyfriend; they had no home so the baby went straight into foster care, and was happily brought up by foster parents for a year – its whole life, in fact.

Mother saw the baby occasionally and had it for the day; whenever she did, the baby came back filthy, nappy unchanged all day and greedily sucking at a bottle of cold tea. She was a violent woman, as her boyfriend testified, and while they

now had a home where there was room for their child, they
had already had a lodger with a recent prison record for
sexually abusing his own children. Hardly a background, you
would think, for justifying taking a one-year-old from a
happy and caring home, and the only people it really knew as
parents.

Unfortunately for the child, there was another factor. The
woman had recently been sterilised and could have no more
children. This settled it for the judge. The woman should have
one final chance to prove that she could be a mother, he
decreed, and the baby should be returned to her. One last
chance for the mother, perhaps, but what sort of chance was
it for the baby?

The local authority that had been responsible for the child
took this judgment to appeal. They could not see how the
judge could have put the child's interests first, as he was
bound in law to do. But the court of appeal upheld the
decision, for reasons which may seem curious but which were
undoubtedly legally proper. The appeal judges made it quite
clear that they were not going to comment on whether they
agreed with what the trial judge had decided; that was not
their job. Their concern was that he had followed the proper
procedures in reaching his decision. I am sure that, in law,
they were right. But I find it hard not to believe that the
decision was wrong, and that it failed to put the child first.
Even had all been well with the natural mother, there would
have been problems for any infant in adjusting to a completely
new environment after the whole of the first year of its life
had been spent in the settled surroundings of the only home
and the only caring relationships it had ever known.

Putting the child first may not be very easy for judges. It is
no less hard for the rest of us. Do we try to protect the child, or
more easily try to protect our own feelings? If we are worried
about what is happening to the child next door, do we try to
do something about it – or feel uncomfortable about telling
tales or being thought a busybody? If we were really
concerned for the child's safety, would we hesitate? Time and
again people only work themselves up to report a problem
because some terrible child death from cruelty has hit the

headlines, yet surely we should never have to wait for a tragedy to happen before we take steps to try to protect a child we know about from what could be a similar tragedy?

The case I have just quoted raises another important concept. The judge may well have had in mind not only the mother's inability to have any further children, her 'last chance' therefore to prove that she could manage to care for her child; he could also have been influenced by the feeling, whether he expressed it or not, that 'blood is thicker than water' – that he believed in the primacy of the blood tie, in the biological parent having first place.

This, understandably, can be an emotive subject. Blood ties are strong. But to a child the overriding importance is that of what is termed the 'psychological parent'. If we look at the matter from an adult viewpoint, we are likely to side with the blood parent. But supposing we consider the child's perspective? Who has nursed, loved, tended, mothered her – for as long as she can remember? Who is the person she *feels*, throughout her being, to be her natural parent? If it is her only relationship, her whole background and security, how can any adult say that, to support the rights of a blood relationship, the child should be taken from all that has meaning in her life?

Fortunately, for most children the 'psychological parent' is also the natural parent, and there is no conflict. But when a child has come to be brought up by someone other than a natural parent, adults should think very hard about breaking a bond that is crucial for the child, because they will be in very grave danger of *not* putting the child's interests first, if they say that the blood bond matters most, and the natural parents have 'the greater right'. Is a parent's right really greater than the child's right to keep a stable, secure, relationship that predominates in its short life?

Believing the Child

Children cannot be protected if there is no belief that they are at risk, so that all of us who care for children, that is who have responsibility for caring for them, must be aware of the risks that exist, and be prepared to face up to them. One aspect of this is to respond to worrying key signs, like changes in behaviour (see page 192); another is to listen to what the child is trying to say and, most importantly, to believe the child.

For generations there have been children being sexually abused in their own homes. Other relatives may have known, but wouldn't, or couldn't believe it. In other cases the likelihood may have seemed so far-fetched that they would find it more acceptable to disbelieve a child than face up to a very gruesome problem. Yet experience across the world all shows that children seldom lie about being subjected to abuse, sexual abuse particularly. Now that adults are beginning to listen, cases of sexual abuse are coming to light in their thousands. It has been happening all the time, but no one would listen before. It just proves how important it is both to listen to and to believe the child, and to give children a chance to express themselves in their own way.

Taking Action

If it has been decided that a child needs protecting, then something needs to be done straight away (see page 194). For a relative, a neighbour, or someone not professionally qualified to deal with child abuse, this means making sure that your concerns are passed on straight away to someone who is. If the risk to the child is immediate, and serious, it may be necessary to call the police, who have powers to act immediately for the child's safety. More often there will be a suspicion of risk which needs to be looked into, and the difficulty will often be in deciding what is best done for the child's safety.

If, after proper investigation, there is demonstrable risk, it is possible to use a Place of Safety Order. This can be granted by a magistrate at any time of day or night, usually on the application of the police, the Social Services Department of a local authority, or the NSPCC. (Strictly speaking, anyone could apply.) Ideally but impractically such an application will not be made until there has been a full case conference and all the professional workers in health, education and social services involved have contributed to the case from their knowledge of the family and assessed all the information available.

It is then up to the local authority to find an appropriate place of safety. This may be in the child's own home, with certain safeguards; or it could be with a relative; there is less likelihood of it being a children's home but still these provide a valued resource; temporary fostering is more common these days, but sometimes can mean travelling quite a long way to find a suitable home; if there is injury, or the need to have a full medical check-up, a hospital provides for the short term at least a very appropriate safe place.

Removal is Always Harmful

Very often a formal order is not needed, because parents agree to voluntary removal to a place providing safety, frequently a hospital. This is not just because they get 'browbeaten into acquiescence by authoritarian social workers', but because many parents know that they have got into a mess, don't know how to get out of it and welcome an intervention that can help them sort themselves out. If relationships have got to a frantic state, letting the child or children go away even for a day or two can help everyone to calm down and work together towards a solution.

In cases such as that of the mother who left her baby in the snow (p. 23) the opportunity to leave baby with a competent minder, just for a weekend, can mean catching up on sleep, easing up on tension and a chance to think rationally towards tackling whatever other problems a particular household may have. Sometimes this can be achieved by admission to hospital, where baby can be fully examined and assessed, with a view to going home again soon unless some condition is revealed which needs more attention.

In such circumstances removal from the home is very short term, and is acceptable to everybody; even so the child will be disturbed by a sudden change in surroundings and in those caring for it. This is something that needs always to be remembered, and obviously very much more so when steps are taken to remove a child for safety for a longer period. However bad the home, however little love and care there may have been, the place that it thinks of as 'home' and those it recognises as its parents, will have been the only surroundings and the only people who matter for that child's whole life, and any removal from that environment will be harmful to that child's sense of belonging, to its most basic security.

The Wisdom of Solomon

Here then is the biggest dilemma of all for those who want to protect children. There are things badly wrong in a child's home (or so you suspect). You are worried that a baby's injuries may have been deliberately inflicted, or that a small child is being sexually abused – but you can't actually prove it. You know that to remove that infant suddenly from the one home that it has ever known will be bound to cause damage and upset which may change its capacity to cope with insecurity for all its life; and you know too that you will be distressing the rest of the family, and perhaps making it impossible to work effectively with the parents if there are lesser problems in childrearing on which they need your help.

At the same time, you know that if you fail to act on your suspicions or part-proven concerns, and do not secure the removal of that child, it may suffer worse abuse; it may even die. Whichever decision you take, the news media will be on to you like vultures if you are wrong. If a child is unnecessarily removed the uproar will be about officious, unfeeling and authoritarian bureaucrats disrupting peaceful families; if it dies when it might have been saved you will be regarded as more guilty than the man or woman who actually caused the death, as an unfeeling incompetent shilly-shallying do-gooder who connived at an infant's death – probably yet another 'worst child abuse death ever' in the words of the trial judge or the crime reporters.

You won't need this lynch mob baying after you, because you will know, and have to live with the thought, that you have let a child down when it was your whole professional commitment to protect it. And while they hound you from your job (or any other job you try to get) they won't give you credit for knowing far better than they what has gone wrong; nor for caring about it. Nor, above all, will they give you credit for having lived for years in the knowledge that sooner or later you would in all good faith make a wrong decision; that every time you take a short cut on a case which does not look too bad, because there are three others in a bulging caseload which you find desperately worrying and want to give more time to, you live with the knowledge that one day just such a case will turn out wrong. And no one will give you credit for all the cases you've got right.

It would try the wisdom of Solomon himself to get the decision right in every case. One is dealing with basic emotions, fraught family situations, unknown factors in people's past behaviour and experience. One is having to judge what a family is like when there is no one visiting, to assess how seriously things are amiss and then to predict how their future behaviour will develop.

All that you can do is your committed best. Use training, skill, experience and caring concern to reach the best decision that you can. Share with colleagues the stresses of what you are doing, using their support and advice; keep that vital balance between indifference and over-involvement of your feelings, and contain the anger you will often feel lest it obscure your judgment. Seek out all the facts that you can and share fully in your investigations; and at case conference, learn from the experience and knowledge of that family of their doctor, nurse, teacher, nursery matron – whoever from the caring professions, police, probation, or any other professional source, has knowledge of that family – and seek their collective view *on what is best in the interests of that child at that time*.

It is very important indeed that this 'multi-disciplinary' approach, this sharing across the professions, is achieved in every case of suspected child abuse. It is demanding, sometimes threatening to individuals who may feel that they are exposing professional weakness to others, but essential for the sake of the child. At the same time, however, someone has to take responsibility and, in the light of case conference findings, take action. The current guidance from central government is that three agencies – social services, the police and the NSPCC – can each take action on their own authority, despite the findings of a case conference, if they think it necessary in the interests of a child's safety. This should not often happen, and it is not meant to be provocative; it is a wise 'belt and braces' added precaution to help to ensure the safety of a child when there is a conflict of view.

The Least Harmful Option

Recently I heard from a colleague who wrote, 'I have always found it helpful to be reminded that there are no ideal solutions, and that what we are actually dealing with are options that do the least harm to the child, rather than the best good.' It is salutory to bear this in mind, if we are not to become arrogant. When facing the dilemma I have outlined, it is important to remember that whilst removal of a child will cause trauma, this option must be balanced against a judgment of what greater harm may result if it is not removed.

There can be alternatives, of course, but often choosing between them reveals pitfalls all the way. If a father has been sexually abusing his child, it can make more sense to remove him and leave the child in its own home with the rest of its family; a remorseful father may agree to do this, or a court may make it a condition of bail. But will he honour the undertaking? Or try to nobble the evidence? (In 1986 Ronald Barton was convicted of murdering his fourteen-year-old daughter so that she could not provide proof of his incestuous acts.) Have you got the right person? The evidence points to sexual abuse, the father seems the obvious person, but it may be another relative, or a regular visitor or baby-sitter, who is the real culprit. Or there may be more than one culprit. The child may not be safe at all.

Certainly one should try not to have to disturb the child, or to remove it from its mother, but the overriding concern must be to make the child safe if there is justified fear of danger. If, after careful investigation and consultation, removal from home seems the most appropriate course, it must be to a *safe* place. That is not always easy to achieve, however, so compounding the dilemma. Most children's homes do a splendid best to make up for not being the natural home, although a few can be rather forbidding; occasionally, though, they can be centres for child abuse – the worst possible option.

More commonly it is a foster home that is used and likewise foster parents strive to provide loving and secure homes to distressed unhappy children; but where the selection process has failed they can cause further suffering. The man I met who had been removed from an abusing home and fostered out – only to have to run away from his foster home because he was being sexually abused (page 36) had the strength to work through the experience and make good. But not everyone can, and the risk is not only of a tragically blighted life, but that such a victim may at an early age turn to child abuse himself.

Does this mean that the outlook is hopeless? Not at all. Every year there are thousands of children for whom the right decisions are taken, and who receive loving care from caring professionals and volunteers in social services and voluntary agencies. Nevertheless there will have been trauma in their young lives, decisions on 'the least bad option' will not always work out right, and while many will have the resilience to get over it, others will have difficulties (which may mean they will cause difficulties to others) for years, or for life. It can be hard to accept, although it is true, that to help the parents in an appalling home to make it 'barely good enough' for the children to stay there can really be a less bad option than removing them to a 'much better home' – particularly if racial, religious, or cultural changes are involved as well.

Self-protection

Every citizen has a duty of care towards the helpless; anyone who is aware of a helpless child being in danger has a responsibility to do something to ensure that that child is protected. This applies particularly, of course, to parents, relatives and others who have special charge of children.

To recapitulate on what I have said before, there are different ways in which we can protect children. One is to avoid, or help them to avoid, dangerous situations, such as being unprotected from the weather, from traffic, from being attacked by animals, or from suspicious-looking strangers. Another is to recognise when specialist help is needed – calling the emergency services by dialling 999 if there is a fire, or an accident, or a child is trapped; promptly going to the doctor if you are worried about your child's health; reporting to the social services or the NSPCC, however shaky it may make you feel, if you think that a child is being abused. Another (which may not always be thought of as protection) is to make sure that a child is provided for – proper food, fresh air and exercise, to ensure a healthy body that can more readily resist illness. Others include having a child immunised against infectious disease; teaching him or her the importance of hygiene, and diet, of kerb drill and road safety, and (worrying as this may be) of learning increasing independence and self-reliance, within clearly stated 'rules'.

As children get older this training to look after themselves must include helping them to protect themselves from abuse – both by strangers and by people known to them – which isn't so comfortable. It is sadly true that 'Not to take sweets from strangers' isn't just as necessary as ever, but more so. This isn't always easy, and a balance has to be struck between alerting children to dangers that they may face, so that they can avoid them if possible or have some idea as to how to handle them if not, and on the other hand worrying children beyond their capacity to accept the concepts of danger that are being described. Judgments need to be made about which there cannot be hard and fast rules. When is a child old enough to be left alone, or in charge of younger children? When can she or he go out alone? Children vary and parents have to adjust their teaching according to the child.

What is fundamental to the safety of children is that all adults should accept their duty to protect; and that for parents and teachers this includes the duty to teach children how to protect themselves. In recent years there have been several developments to help adults to this end.

Perhaps the most comprehensive package available at this time is produced by Kidscape, which was developed by

Michele Elliott and her colleagues. Intended for parents and for use in schools it provides information, guidance and practical examples of how teachers can develop a programme for children which will promote their personal safety. It teaches children positive practical ways to keep safe from various dangers including sexual abuse. It builds a child's confidence, it engages them in exploring their rights which will include control of their own bodies and it reassures them that some secrets do not need to be kept; some secrets are bad. It equips the child with a strategy for their own protection.

Michelle has also written a book entitled *Keeping Safe*, a practical guide to talking with children, which looks in detail at how parents can help their children remain safe. Written in a non-sensational, low-key way, it also has chapters relating to how teachers may become constructively involved.

Child Protection programmes developed within schools must of course involve the parents who need to consent to the children taking part. In fact it is often the Parent-Teacher Association which initiates these programmes.

The use of personal safety programmes was pioneered in the USA. Gradually the need was identified for British versions and in time these were made. One such video made in 1985 was *Strong Kids Safe Kids*, an adaptation of an American video of the same title, produced with the support of staff from the National Children's Home. Aimed at parents, it endeavoured to teach their children to protect themselves against sexual molestation or abduction, and it was presented through the television character 'the Fonz' with cartoon characters and songs also involved. Like many of these videos it was not intended to be viewed once only but rather to be stopped at strategic places so that parents could discuss the video with their children.

The NSPCC were involved with Skippon Video Associates in producing a short video to be used in schools aimed at the 5–11-year-old age group. This too was not intended to be used independently but rather should involve teachers in the process of discussion with children. Rolf Harris features in this particular programme and he is seen talking to a group of 7–8-year-olds about 'yes' feelings and 'no' feelings. It goes on to demonstrate situations in which children might be in danger from both strangers and people they know and trust, and to suggest ways to prevent harm and how they might explain what has happened to them to a caring adult.

The key to effective work in the field of personal safety for children is gaining their trust and conveying simple messages. The particular strength of Kidscape is that it involves teachers or facilitators and the information is conveyed through a relationship with the adult who is able to be responsive to the needs of children.

In 1987 it became evident to the NSPCC that parents were unsure about how to protect their children and were found to be questioning their own relationships with the child. Events in Cleveland had undermined some parents' confidence and we had been asked such questions as 'Is it all right if I cuddle my child?' or 'Is it proper for a father to bath the children?' Very natural and spontaneous affection was being questioned. In the face of this confusion it was determined to provide simple and appropriate reassurance and in 1987 the NSPCC produced a booklet for parents which was widely distributed free of charge. Over a million copies were available through a range of outlets in the community planned to reach all parents.

Whilst the NSPCC was concerned about the increase in reports of sexual abuse to children, the majority of parents do not molest their children and are anxious to protect them from such experiences. Recognising these parents' need for reassurance, enabling them to be more confident in their role and in carrying out their responsibilities, the booklet answered simple questions such as: What are the early warning signs of sexual abuse? Can I touch my child? How can I help my child overcome abuse? Will my child be taken away? Can my child be medically examined without my consent? What will happen to the offender?

There is quite a considerable amount of other material available now to help parents and teachers with the task of protecting their children. (If the reader wishes to know more about this, information is available through the NSPCC Library.) The task is a vital part of the adult's responsibility to the child.

Chapter 11: **The Prevention of Cruelty**

Despite all that is said and written about the 'overriding need to prevent all kinds of child abuse and neglect', we must be realistic. Human nature will continue to be human nature, every one of us is capable of doing evil in one form or another, and whatever we try to do there will be some people who perform malicious acts, some who are deliberately cruel, some who lose their tempers and do violent things they later regret and some who make grave errors of judgment which may have untoward effects on other people or on their own children.

No amount of religious leadership, legislation or police provision has halted the occurrence of unlawful killings – of adults or of children. Rigorous and excessive chastisement has been noticeable in some parents of apparently impeccable standing in civic and church affairs. The same appears at times to be the case with grosser forms of abuse, such as sexual molestation. Child injuries occur not only as the result of deliberate acts that were intended to harm, but also through more force being used than was intended; as when shaking a child, or angrily giving what is meant to be a light blow, but which was never meant to cause permanent disability from brain damage.

This demonstrates that absolute prevention is unattainable, but it does not mean for a moment that prevention should be regarded as hopeless. There are many things which can be done to make child abuse less prevalent and its occurrence less burdensome to the victims.

Immediately, we are faced by two dilemmas. The first is

that, as I have said, however much one may want to tackle the root problems, there is a conflict of priorities; it may be more important to concentrate on long-term preventive measures, but it is undoubtedly more urgent to respond to immediate crises where children are at risk.

The other dilemma is this. Responding to a child abuse emergency, as to a fire, or as to a medical crisis, has demonstrable, sometimes dramatic, results, and can be verified and costed. The same costs devoted to a preventive programme might prevent many more cases from ever becoming emergencies, but this cannot be proved. People who allocate funds like to see provable results; if they are politicians, local or national, they like to see those results soon enough to have electoral significance (whereas much basic prevention is far longer term) – and they prefer tangible effects. Newsmen, who can apply the pressure on politicians, prefer drama: one picture of a badly battered baby will have front-page coverage in every tabloid newspaper; pictures of a hundred happy babies who did not suffer abuse after a preventive programme will not. Somehow a balance needs to be struck between three types of prevention, which can include (as defined by the NSPCC) 'Stage 3 prevention' – preventing it from happening again; 'Stage 2 prevention', – identifying and helping those most at risk; and 'Stage 1 prevention' – trying to avoid, or at least minimise, the development of 'at risk' categories.

Preventing It From Happening Again

The first priority when child abuse is suspected must be to ensure the safety of the child or children concerned and this protective response, which is so essential in its provision of a thoroughly professional investigation, has the third stage of prevention implied as well – to protect the child from any further abuse. This is why a readiness to respond as a matter of urgency to allegations of children being at risk is very necessary, and why it must be linked to the skill and commitment of investigative work by the primary worker, and the professional sharing of everybody who can contribute to establishing the facts. The reason is twofold: it is essential to establish whether there is anything wrong, and, if so, to be clear what it is so that appropriate action can be taken in order to prevent the abuse from continuing.

When the whole attitude of a family may be to conceal a child abuse problem from investigators, or parents are unwilling to accept that it is taking place at all, a particular strain is placed upon child abuse workers. While they must avoid false accusations, they must also avoid being manipulated into accepting an adult view which is misleading. The first step in prevention is proper investigation: how *could* an injured baby of that age have hurt himself by 'climbing out of his cot'? The living room looks fine – but what are the children's bedrooms like? The explanation of a bruise on baby's face may be acceptable – but are there any other bruises elsewhere on its body?

The next step to take is that of treating and involving the whole family. The problem that has come to light may be an isolated incident, it may focus on one child only; there may, however, be other factors which cause the stress and these may be the behaviour of the other parent, other children or others in the household. A mother who is not coping adequately with her tasks, a single parent trying to hold down a job and manage a demanding family, may need support; this can be provided in a variety of ways, as has been illustrated earlier in this book. Self-help groups can have a valuable role to play. The health visitor or clinic can help with teaching management of proper care, nursing, hygiene and nutrition. Through organised groups parents can learn to lose their feelings of isolation, identify their problems, and come to realise how to tackle them and be supported by the group in doing so.

The most fundamental resource in work with the family is the casework relationship; the relationship the worker develops with the family. It is the worker who will confront the family with the need for change and by use of varying techniques and resources try to effect necessary movement building upon the positive features of the family members, particularly the adults.

Family centres and other forms of day care can play an immensely useful role, and their significance is growing as this is recognised and skills are developed in using their resources. A mother can feel trapped in her home, which can lead to resentment which boils over at a minor incident, such as some food being brought up on the crest of an infant burp. Taking her baby to a centre is an outing and it means companionship and support from staff who are welcoming and understanding.

The staff can also help with training in responsibility and domestic skills. Mothers can improve their cooking by taking it in turns to help in the centre's kitchen. They can develop other skills by sharing in the bathing and changing of their own and other children, washing, mending and ironing, and they can learn how to shop, budget, plan meals and share their different skills in making clothes and toys and playing with the children. A mother who wants a break from the children can go and relax in the 'parents only' room – but not by just hoping that someone else will keep an eye on her own child(ren); she must make arrangements for someone else to be responsible for her family, and her peers will soon pick her up if she doesn't. For children, there are opportunities at family centres for them to develop through play and companionship; and their weights and developmental land-marks can be monitored.

Likewise if a child seems to regress, to go back into his or her shell, or show other changes in behaviour which are worrying, it may mean that a crisis is building up at home, and that the social worker should be alerted. Using day-care facilities in ways which can be so positive for the development of parents and children has many advantages in providing a complete preventive and developmental programme which can help a whole family to make progress; additionally there can be this most useful protective monitoring of children who have been abused, and who may still be at risk. Day care can be a desirable alternative to placing a child in residential care, and costs less in emotional trauma and disruption of relation-ships, as well as in cash. Its facilities can also be used to give monitoring and support when children come out of residential care, as a 'halfway house' facility which can shorten the period that families are apart, when they are not totally ready to manage on their own, or when it is too risky just to assume that they are.

Family centres may have a use for fathers too. There may be genuine reasons, such as his job, which make it more difficult for a man to take part in day-centre activities; there are also cultural ones which make him less likely to want to. But as perceptions of roles within marriage become less rigid, and marriage is increasingly seen as a partnership where the activities in bringing up a family are better shared, so one sees fathers attending family centres, and able to benefit themselves, and have their own group activities.

The preventive role of suitable centres can go further, when they are structured not only to provide support and assessment for individual members and groups, but also for assessments of a whole family. One of the most difficult questions to be faced is that of deciding whether a home where there has been serious, or repeated, child abuse or neglect should continue, or whether permanent alternative care is necessary. Making this decision can be helped by inviting the whole family to come together, perhaps while the children are in temporary foster care, or the father is staying in a hostel, so as to explore how well they get on with each other. If the children have not seen their father for some time, how do they react and how does he react when he comes into the room? Is there joy, indifference, apprehension? Do they play together? Is there a basis on which one can build and work towards keeping that family together? Or are attitudes and antipathies such that the children need to be given a fresh start in another relationship? A family centre is an ideal place to undertake work which answers these questions.

Where the signs are promising there may need to be sustained effort on everybody's part, so that parents who have failed can regain their confidence and gain insight into their own behaviour and understanding of their children, so that the circumstances and attitudes which led to abuse or neglect are not repeated. If this is really to be an effective preventive exercise it is also necessary that parents learn to be independent, rather than function well only when they can depend upon professional staff being 'in charge'. They have got to be in charge of themselves, and able to demonstrate to themselves and to the staff that they can be, and want to be, in charge of running their families. They not only need to be set goals that they can achieve; they may need to learn to accept the responsibility of agreeing to, and observing, a 'contract' with the staff.

Whether using day-care facilities in this way or not, professional workers have to set up targets, and in many instances will indeed develop written contracts, so that they agree to provide stated facilities for a set period, provided that the parents undertake to achieve certain landmarks in developing family management skills, and so show that they are keen to move towards greater independence and develop self-confidence in providing a real and caring home for their children. For example, an achievement in cleaning and redecorating the home, or in learning to provide simple satisfying meals, might be rewarded by arranging a family holiday.

Working With 'At Risk' Groups

We have been looking at the preventive aspect of dealing with families where abuse or neglect (or grave risk of such) have already been identified: there is a problem which needs attention, and circumstances need to be altered if the desired goal of that family staying together is to be achieved and further risk for the children is to be avoided. But before abuse occurs there is the stage when there is a risk of abuse developing; and an important aim in the prevention of abuse is to try to identify those families where the risk of abuse is most likely, so that you can take action to forestall it happening.

Staff are limited in numbers, and the cost of preventive programmes can be high. There is therefore much to be said for focusing upon the most important target groups in order to do the most good with the resources that there are; the alternative can all too easily be to spread the educational and training provisions so thinly across the whole population that little good is done to anyone, and those with most need do not get most attention.

Chapter 2 discussed how child abuse happens, and how it was possible to try to identify characteristics of children, parents and families, which might make abuse a more likely occurrence. If one can identify the prodromal characteristics, one can more easily take steps to forestall the harm which is more likely to befall children in such families than in the normal population.

We have seen how there can be young mothers who have not the least experience of fun with their children, who do not know how to love, who have never learned to play; parents who do not know what to expect of their children, and who in seeing unrealistic expectations not being met, may react by rejecting their children, or subjecting them to punitive violence or neglect.

So often families like this are isolated, far from their own parents or in-laws, or alienated from them, and through their behaviour and appearance tend to be shunned by their neighbours. One way to help this problem might be to establish a task force – 'Rentagranny' volunteers – who would be able to adopt a family and help in practical ways, and with motherly advice, about parentcraft skills and household management. Perhaps, too, there should be greater focus upon promoting the development of self-help groups for young parents, or parents-to-be, which would help them through group-sharing to learn how to develop in their own relationships, and how to understand and respond to the needs of their children. There can be no doubt that self-help groups can do immense good and achieve considerable preventive value. Self-help playgroups too can be a way of helping children to mix and learn to share, as well as companionship for parents, some of whom need to learn how to mix and share as well.

Trying to tackle child abuse in this way bears out the experience of Dr Jack Dominian, that wise counsellor in marital breakdown. Many years ago I heard Dr Dominian address a gathering concerned with the high rate of failure in marriages, that 'time-bomb under society' as the Bishop of

Worcester described it, by challenging whether the search for better remedial measures was the right way to tackle the problem. If so many marriages are breaking down, Dr Dominian argued, rather than placing emphasis upon re-cruiting and training more counsellors to help those whose lives had come apart, it might be better to help those embarking upon married life to achieve greater strength and understanding in their relationship the one with the other, so that there was less likelihood of breakdown.

This positive, preventive approach appealed to me very much. It is so simple; if a structure of any sort keeps breaking down, it is better to create a stronger structure in the first place than keep trying to patch it up. When I joined the NSPCC I had this example very much in mind when looking at the problems of child abuse, which are indeed so often linked to marital discord – the most common single underlying factor, as we have seen.

Unfortunately, as we have also seen, the predictive factors by which one can identify those families that are most at risk of potential child abuse and neglect are not precise enough. Housing problems can add to the stress within a family; tensions can build up when there is overcrowding, discomfort, bad plumbing, poor facilities. But thousands of people have housing problems, and while there may be too much burden for parents reasonably to bear, only a small proportion of them will let the children suffer.

Financial problems can be a constant drain on a family, and how to tackle them a source of disagreement and recrimination; yet when money is short, most couples resolve that the children should be the last to suffer. The different aspects of what is lumped together as the single problem of unemploy-ment have been explored already; the stress of fearing that one's job may go; the shock when it does; the growing feeling of worthlessness when unemployment goes on and on – these all have effects which can be very profound on how a family can hold together. But again it must be said that with both parents at home the care of the children can be shared, the standards can improve; it is only in some households that the children become victims.

With the great upsurge in the discovery of cases of sexual abuse in children, it has become clear that a great deal of it is perpetrated by men who had themselves been sexually assaulted when they were young; they are also likely to have many victims. Yet only a minority of those victims will themselves become abusers. It is impossible to predict which and focus on their needs.

To produce special child abuse prevention schemes for all couples with marital problems, for all families where there is unemployment, for everyone with housing difficulties, emotional problems, financial crises, isolation from other relatives, or other named stresses and insecurities would rather take the 'special' out of what would be broadly focused on millions of people, most of whom would not be in danger of abusing their children. Probably most of them could gain some benefit – indeed we could all improve as parents – but the inability that we have at present to be able to be more precise in predicting high-risk households means that a high-powered close-focus campaign cannot be achieved.

There are certain circumstances when prediction can be made at an individual level. A midwife, for instance, can tell from the flat, indifferent, uncaring attitude of some pregnant patients that this indifference might well extend to caring for the baby when it is born; she might have all the more dramatic cause for concern at the time of birth if the normal joy and tenderness shown by a young mother as her new-born baby is first placed in her arms is undeniably absent. Such observations are important, and need to be passed on so that special provision can be made; important, but only reaching a limited sector of the problem. How, for example, can you discern which happy young mother who loves her baby will have a husband who doesn't?

Another problem that is by no means unique to the need to identify and provide special education for potential child abusers is the risk that those most in need will take no part, and that those who do respond to parentcraft programmes will be those whose concern to be good parents shows them to be least in need of preventive strategies.

Avoiding the Development of 'At-Risk' Categories: Preparation for Parenthood

The fact that we do not know enough about how to identify the key factors in predicting potential abusers does not mean that we should abandon the attempt. It is highly probable that not enough resources have been devoted to the subject. While it is undoubtedly true that there are so many variables, such idiosyncrasies in individual human reactions, that the task is formidable, the task is not impossible; it just takes longer and requires more humility in accepting our limitations, and our tendencies to look for quick and easy explanations. We must continue to look for other things to do to help.

To me, the most fundamental area of prevention, taking a leaf from Dr Dominian's book, is in the basic education of our children. At a time when the whole school curriculum is coming under examination it may be timely to press this point of view. 'Education' has a Latin derivation that means 'leading forward', which implies a whole lot more than the necessary teaching that is implicit in the standard school syllabus. Educating children means preparing them for adult life.

Of course, children need to learn skills in communicating, thinking, managing computers and other modern technology, so that they can cope as adults in this modern world, get jobs, play sports, use their leisure and so forth. But this is not all they need if they are to be 'led forward' into adult life. For adult life is also about coping with oneself, with developing (or messing up) relationships with others, with achieving lasting pairing with the right person and having a family, and knowing how to manage running a home and bringing up children.

Yet while there is more and more technology devoted – rightly – to teaching workaday skills related to jobs, not so much time is given to helping young people to learn about relationships. Young people need to receive help in learning about their own development, in achieving understanding of their inner selves as they make the confused and sometimes stormy transition through adolescence into adulthood. They need to be offered understanding into relationships amongst themselves, girl with boy, boy with girl. They need preparation for their role as parents and instruction in home management, including the dietary and developmental needs of children. They need an understanding of the joys, and the stresses, of family life. But our education system is woefully inadequate in providing any of these things.

It seems to me extraordinary how parenthood, the bringing up of the next generation, which is surely the most important task that most of us can perform, should be left to the happenstance of our own upbringing, and how we as individuals apply that to our children. We are taught to read, write, add, work word processors; but in learning to be wives, or husbands, or parents, we are left entirely to our own devices. Then hands are raised in pious horror if we get it wrong!

That may not matter for those of us who had an abundance of love, and understanding, unselfish and farseeing parents. We have a good model to follow, and a knowledge that love has redeeming qualities when crises arise. But what of those who have had no such security in their upbringing? This is not a matter of social grading, or income level. Whatever the material well-being, it is the richness, or the poverty, of spirit within a household that makes the difference between it being a house and a home.

It is true that there are those who, however rich and warm their upbringing, manage to belie their experience and fail in their own family life; there are also others who, despite miserable childhoods, rise above such experience to offer a richness of love and thoughtfulness to the next generation. For most of us, though, the tendency is to carry on the tradition to which we were introduced, for better or for worse. It seems wrong that the happiness and effectiveness of the upbringing of the next generation of children should rest on so haphazard a basis.

I held forth in these terms to the headmaster of a well-known school for boys, who disagreed with me about developing parenthood topics within the school curriculum. He felt that pupils would not be prepared to respond to what they were not yet interested in. Funnily enough, and unknown to him, I was invited to speak to senior pupils at his school a little while later. I spoke on this subject, in the context of the unhappiness which could exist in many homes because parents did not know how to cope, although they usually wanted to. I do not think that I have ever had a more attentive audience.

The questions that flowed at the end of my talk showed that the pupils had great interest in the subject, and the relevance of their questions demonstrated that had I been unrealistic in anything I said they would soon have shown me up. These young people knew – as so many of their contemporaries know – of the misery and unkindness borne by some of their classmates. They *knew* of the need to be able to understand how to raise a family and they wanted to learn more.

I spoke on this topic again (I often do) when opening the NSPCC Family Craft Centre. There was a senior policeman among the guests, who talked to me afterwards. He and his wife had offered themselves as foster parents, and asked for placements of particularly difficult or awkward children, because they felt that they had the security and experience to be able to cope better than many who might be nervous of dealing with a troublesome teenager.

He told me that currently they had a teenage girl with them with a troubled history, and who had been found to be educationally subnormal. In fact they had found that this girl responded so well to being in a caring and understanding home that it rapidly became apparent that she was not educationally subnormal at all. She had been 'emotionally subnormal' – so withdrawn and uncommunicative from the psychological trauma in her natural home that it was not until she began to relax, trust and feel secure that she could release her emotions and begin to catch up with her development and show her capacity for normal schooling.

However, what my superintendent friend particularly wanted to share with me was the fact that while this girl was at a special school, the curriculum for the subnormal had included classes labelled 'Parenthood', but they seemed to be entirely focused on sex education: they included nothing about learning how to be grown-up, marry, share lives together, care for children.

And it is not that there is any lack of wanting to learn. An NSPCC worker, who made a point of giving talks in schools about the challenges and problems of parenthood, had such attentive audiences that she sought the aid of the video unit of the local health authority, and with them created a teaching tape. She knew that the teenage pupils were fully aware that abuse and neglect happened – they could see it in their own communities – and she was anxious to help them to develop attitudes that would help them later when they were setting up for themselves. Even if it may be too early to give instruction in certain skills and they may quickly be forgotten, an understanding of the fact that there are needs and ways of meeting them, as well as facilities for learning and getting help, could be put across.

Young people face enormous pressures these days, with the instant communication, instant gratification of wants, that is presented to them in attractive packaging by the commercial interests that want their money. They need a chance to learn how to cope, with themselves and their partners; to realise that babies are not just those flaxen-haired little darlings which gurgle so delightfully from the television advertise-ments – and which can be switched off by remote control!

In real life babies can be delightful, but they are there all the time and need attention, whether they are teething in the middle of the night, or making a mess at the most awkward moment, or needing costly expenditure just when the car needs repair and the gas bill has come in. The NSPCC worker's amateur video showed these things, with interviews with young parents talking about their pleasures in having children, and also the difficulties, which had often come because they were not prepared for them. 'It cost much more than we realised,' said one couple; 'You can't just go out in the evening,' said another; 'you either have to get a baby-sitter or stay in.'

The effect of the video upon school audiences was interest-ing. The girl who wanted a professional career did not feel deterred from wanting a family as well, but she realised that she would have to think out how she set about it. The lad who wanted a large family still did, but said, 'There's more to having a family than I realised; you have to think about it.' It is the establishment of these attitudes – that there is a responsibility to the children in having a family; that one has to think out the implications and be ready for them; that one has to be prepared to be a parent – that is so necessary.

I am not sure that it is ever too young to start. I had a charming letter from the headmistresses of two primary schools who had been to a seminar by some of my staff about preparation for parenthood being necessary as an integral part of the curriculum; it should not, as so often happens with sex education, be something treated as 'different' and isolated from everything else, but be a normal facet of growing up and a natural part of what is taught in school. These two ladies wrote to say that they had gone to the meeting out of general interest in the topic, not feeling that it had any relevance to the age of child they were responsible for. However, they had come away after the session enthused with the relevance of what had been discussed, and excited by the realisation that even at primary school there was scope for children to start learning about family life and reponsibilities in a way that could either reinforce, or compensate for, their own experience.

Audiences across the country seem to respond to this simple message. A whole range of organisations that try to deal with the ill-effects of marital and family breakdown have a shared interest in putting better foundations into the building of understanding, relationships, readiness for responsibility, preparedness to understand and response to the needs of children in body, mind and spirit. When will something be done about it that can start some movement in the real work of preventing cruelty to children – teaching those who are prepared to learn how to be good parents?

The most important investment we can have is in the upbringing of the next generation, and their development to face the responsibilities they will inherit. The trauma, the suffering, the sheer waste and human misery that are demonstrated in child abuse and neglect reflect the inability of some parents – many thousands of parents – to understand their children's needs, or to respect their rights, or to give them the basis of love and caring that they need. There are many more families where demonstrable cruelty may not happen, but where the quality of nurturing is borderline, and there are few where bringing up the family might not be improved – especially with the firstborn, at whose expense so much may be learned.

The fundamental need is to regard education for adult relationships and parental management of child-rearing as an imperative if all children in the next generation are to have the opportunity, whatever the quality of their own upbringing, to raise the standards of parentcraft for future generations. We can never eradicate all cruelty, but we can substantially reduce the ignorance, the lack of understanding of the child's viewpoint and the child's needs, which so often are demonstrated today.

Child abuse is a family problem, but it is a community concern. How concerned is our community to put the right energy and resources into preparing the children of today for their role as the parents of tomorrow?

Appendix I: **Child Protection Law**

The government published far-reaching proposals to reform child care law in January 1987. It is intended that new legislation will be introduced as soon as the parliamentary timetable allows. At present the principal statutes which contain powers to protect children from abuse or neglect are the Children and Young Persons Act 1933, the Children and Young Persons Act 1969 and the Child Care Act 1980. These provide procedures:

(a) for children to be admitted into care voluntarily if their parents are unable to care for them
(b) for children to be taken into care compulsorily if they have been abused or neglected or are at risk of abuse
(c) for children to be removed from home to a place of safety for a specified period as an emergency measure.

Voluntary Care

Under s.2 of the Child Care Act 1980 a local authority has a duty to receive into care any child under seventeen years who has been abandoned or whose parents cannot properly care for him because of illness, incapacity or for any other reason. Reception into care is voluntary and a local authority cannot intervene and remove a child from home under this provision without parental consent. A parent can remove the child from care at any time but must give twenty-eight days' notice if the child has been in care for the preceding six months. Voluntary care should be viewed as a temporary remedy and whenever possible the local authority must try to ensure that the child's care is resumed or taken over by a parent, guardian, relative or friend provided this is consistent with his welfare.

Compulsory Care

1. A parental rights resolution
In certain cases it may not be in a child's interests to return home after a period in voluntary care. To prevent this a local authority may pass a resolution under s.3 of the Child Care Act 1980 assuming

the parental rights and duties of one or both parents of a child in voluntary care. The effect of this is to deprive a parent of all the usual parental rights including the right to remove the child from care. A resolution can be passed only:

(a) if a parent is dead or his whereabouts have been unknown for at least a year since the child came into care, or
(b) if the child has been in care throughout the preceding three years, or
(c) if a parent is unfit to care for the child by reason of permanent disability, mental disorder, unsuitable habits and modes of life or a consistent failure to discharge his parental obligations without reasonable cause, or
(d) if there is already a resolution in force in relation to one parent who is or is likely to become a member of the same household as the child and the other parent.

A parent may object to a resolution depriving him of parental rights. The local authority must then apply to a juvenile court for the resolution to be confirmed otherwise it will lapse. The court may confirm the resolution if the grounds are proved and it is in the child's interests to do so. A resolution will last until the child is eighteen years old unless it is revoked by the local authority. A parent can apply to a juvenile court for its early discharge. The court will only discharge a resolution if satisfied that there were no grounds for passing it or that discharge would now be in the child's interests.

2. A care order

A juvenile court may commit a child to the care of a local authority if satisfied that one of the grounds set out in s.1(2)(a)–(f) of the Children and Young Persons Act 1969 is proved and that the child is in need of care or control which he is unlikely to receive unless an order is made. The grounds relate either to the child's present condition or to a potential risk to which he may be exposed. They are:

(a) that the child's proper development is being avoidably prevented or neglected, or his health is being avoidably impaired or neglected or he is being ill-treated, or
(b) It is probable that the above condition will apply because

   (i) it has applied to another child who is or was a member of the same household, or

(ii) a person who has been convicted of an offence against a child is or may become a member of the same household as the child

(c) that he is exposed to moral danger
(d) that he is beyond parental control
(e) that he is of compulsory school age and is not receiving efficient full-time education suitable to his age, ability and aptitude
(f) that he is guilty of an offence excluding homicide.

Care proceedings may be brought by a local authority, the police or the NSPCC. If the case is proved the court may make one of the following orders:

a care order committing the child to the care of a local authority until the age of eighteen years and effectively transferring to the local authority parental rights and duties including the right to decide where the child will live

a supervision order placing the child under the supervision of a local authority or a probation officer for a maximum period of three years

a hospital order or *a guardianship order* providing treatment for a mentally disordered child

an order requiring a parent to enter into a *recognisance* to take proper care of the child.

A parent can apply to the juvenile court on the child's behalf for variation or discharge of a care order or supervision order.

3. Wardship
Wardship is a process whereby the court can take over the legal powers of a parent.

The High Court can commit a ward of court to the care of a local authority if there are exceptional circumstances making it impracticable or undesirable for the child to be in the care of either parent or any other parent. The principal consideration for the court is the welfare of the child which is paramount. A local authority may make a child a ward of court and seek a care order when there are no grounds to pass a parental rights resolution or to apply to the juvenile court for a care order but the child is nevertheless at risk.

4. Care orders in other proceedings
Care orders can be made in adoption and custody proceedings to prevent a child from coming into the care of a parent or any other

person considered undesirable by the court. They can also be made in criminal proceedings when a child has committed an offence.

Emergency Measures

It may be necessary to remove a child from home quickly as an emergency measure. Under s.28(1) of the Children and Young Persons Act 1969 any person may apply to a single magistrate for authority to detain a child under seventeen years in a place of safety for up to twenty-eight days. This procedure is used principally by social workers and officers of the NSPCC. Application may be made outside court hours at a magistrate's home. It is not necessary for the child or parent(s) to be present. The applicant must have reasonable cause to believe that one of the grounds for bringing care proceedings is satisfied or that a court would find it probable that the child will be ill-treated because this has happened to another child in the same household. There is no appeal against a place of safety order. When the order expires the child must be returned home unless an application has been made to a juvenile court for an interim care order. An interim care order can last a maximum of twenty-eight days. If care proceedings are commenced under the Children and Young Persons Act 1969, s.1 the court can make further interim care orders until the final hearing of the case.

A police officer can detain a child in a place of safety without a magistrate's order for up to eight days provided that detention is authorised by a senior officer. If it is necessary to search premises for a child a magistrate can issue a warrant under s.40 of the Children and Young Persons Act 1933 authorising a police officer to search named premises and remove the child if necessary. A warrant can provide for a doctor to accompany a police officer, if necessary.

A place of safety can be a children's home, a foster home, a police station, a hospital, a surgery or any other place willing to receive a child. A parent cannot appeal against a place of safety order or warrant but he can apply to a magistrate on the child's behalf for release from police detention.

Further Reading

Brenda Hoggett, *Parents and Children* Sweet and Maxwell; Roger Smith, *Children and the Courts* Sweet and Maxwell; *Child Care Legislation – a Guide for Social Workers*, Community Care; *A Guide to Care Proceedings* Family Rights Group, 6–9 Manor Gdns, Holloway Rd, London N7 6LA; B. I. Slomnicka, *Law of Child Care* Macdonald & Evans; Jean Graham Hall and Douglas F. Martin, *Child Abuse – Procedure and Evidence in Juvenile Courts* Barry Rose; *Clarke Hall and Morrison on Children*, (10th Edition) Butterworths; Linda Feldman, *Care Proceedings* Oyez Longman

I am grateful to Linda Feldman of the NSPCC's legal section for producing Appendix I.

Appendix II: **Steps Taken Following Concern That a Child May Be Abused or Neglected**

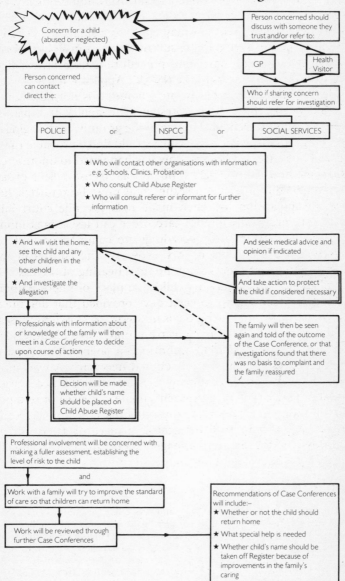

Physical Neglect – Checklist for a Home Visit by Social Worker or Health Worker

When first visiting a home judgments will need to be made and these must take account of socio-economic norms for the neighbourhood and cultural background of the family.

Observations will be in the context of referral information – what is alleged or suspected? Of whom? By whom? When? How? Over what period? Who was said to be involved?

The Home (all rooms, especially bedrooms, should be seen)

Condition of the garden, windows, curtains, decoration

Overall appearance and condition: cleanliness, warmth, smell, state of furnishings

Adequacy of domestic services: gas, electricity, water, hot water supply

Condition of WC, cooking area, baby food preparation facilities, cleanliness etc.

Sufficient beds, adequate dry bedding

Obvious soiling (urine saturation, presence of faeces)

Safety provisions: fireguards, stairgate, electric sockets, cooker-guard, (proper electrical plugs,) dangerous windows, broken glass, lighting

Presence and availability of appropriate toys and play materials (beware the too-tidy house)

Adequate food

The Adults (including non-parents)

State of preparedness for the time of day (are they out of bed, use of alcohol, addictive substances etc)

Who is in the home – does it provide stability?

Nature of interaction between adults: evidence of marital disharmony

Degree of passiveness, level of intelligence

Isolation in their community

The Children (see *all* the children of the family)

Adequacy and appropriateness of clothing for activities and climate

State of cleanliness, hygiene, hair care

Physical frailty, size or ill health (if not well what help or advice and how sought)

Pattern of feeding – confirm by calling at meal times and seeing food being prepared

Pattern of school attendance – corroboration by school authorities

Observed developmental level (walking, speaking, toilet training)

Nature of interaction with other family members especially adults (including demeanour)

Beware of the apprehensive child and over-compliance

Warmth of relationship with parent – look for encouragement and approval (note wariness)

Nature of behaviour, handling i.e. correction outweighing encouragement

Attitude to observer

Ask about any observed injuries

Background History

Family history of parents (background – including poverty, abuse, harsh discipline, absence of discipline)

Adults having current or past 'nervous' or mental illness problems

Adults having current or past 'anti-social' problems especially offences involving violence

Alcohol-related problems

Problems with other children

Repeated injuries and accidents to children (other than recognised non-accidental injury)

Money management – debts, evictions, services cut off, HP reclamations, gambling, excessive drinking (does story match what is observed?)

Support available from neighbours and extended family (how isolated are family, what is the subculture?)

For specific child: unwanted pregnancy, history of feeding problems or sleeping difficulties

Additional Features Relating to Surgery/Hospital Visits

Attitude of child to professionals

Discrepancies and intentionally misleading features in parents' accounts

Unjustifiable non-attendance at clinics for appointments

Attitude to/degree of compliance with professional advice

Response of parents to visit

Appendix IV: **How Should I Help My Child to Avoid Child Abuse?**

Prevention is better than cure and parents can do a great deal to protect their children. This will require building up a trusting and open relationship between you and your child. Talking about danger can be difficult and take time but if it prevents your child being abused it will be worth it.

What you tell your child will depend on his or her age but even young children can understand very simple messages, such as not talking to strangers and not going off with strangers and not agreeing to do things they are unhappy about. Your child can understand that while there are some exciting secrets, there are also some that are 'bad' and these should not be kept.

You can drawn up a 'code' to help protect your child. It might include:

That you always believe your children and help them. They should not be worried about telling you anything.

If they don't need to be accompanied by an adult, children should, wherever possible, go around in pairs or in groups. They should always take a pre-arranged route home.

A young child should not be allowed to go to public places such as lavatories on his or her own.

Baby-sitters and child minders will be thoroughly checked to see if they are totally reliable and can be trusted.

Children should know that they can do anything they like when they are in danger and someone is hurting or threatening to hurt them – run away, scream, shout, kick, punch or lie. Their safety is all that matters.

Children should remember the three 'W's' and tell you:
WHO they are going out with.
WHERE they are going.
WHEN they are going to be home.

Children can choose for themselves who they want to kiss, cuddle and hug them. They shouldn't be made to do these things against their will, particularly if they feel it is wrong.

In short, you will need to talk about the dangers of abuse to your children in a way that is appropriate to their age. It is not necessary to use the term 'sexual abuse' with young children nor to talk about it in a way that is frightening to them. If you become aware that your child has been abused get him help immediately and support your child, assure them that they are not to blame.

Appendix V: **Sexual Abuse – What are the Early Warning Signs?**

The suffering of sexually abused children shows most frequently in the way they behave.

Unlike physical abuse where the signs are often quite obvious, those of sexual abuse are seldom evident. In many cases any evidence that the child has been abused can disappear in a few days, and many forms of abuse (fondling, oral sex) do not normally leave physical signs. It is the adult's responsibility to try to understand how the child feels and what is happening.

Below are listed some of the ways children can, and do, show their distress. Whilst these signs do not necessarily mean that a child has been abused (there could be other and very valid explanations for a child behaving in these ways) they could indicate that the child is being sexually abused and needs help:

aggressive behaviour, severe tantrums

an air of 'detachment' or 'don't care' attitude

overly compliant behaviour, 'watchful' attitude

sexually explicit behaviour (e.g. playing games and showing awareness which is inappropriate for the child's age)

continual open masturbation, aggressive and inappropriate sex play

the child seems happy only in school – or is kept away from school by a parent

does not join in school activities, has few school friends

does not trust adults, particularly those who are close

'tummy pains' with no medical reason

eating problems, including over-eating, loss of appetite

disturbed sleep, nightmares, bedwetting

running away from home, suicide attempts, self-inflicted wounds

reverting to young behaviour, depression, withdrawal

relationships between adults and children which are secretive and exclude others.

If you feel or suspect that your child is being abused you need to seek help and advice now.

Index